TABLE OF C

HOW TO

STOP
CARING
WHAT
OTHERS
THINK

FOR REAL.

SHONA SCHWARTZ

HOW TO STOP CARING WHAT OTHERS THINK FOR REAL.

Shona Schwartz

This publication is designed to provide accurate and authoritative information in regard to the subject matter covered. It is sold with the understanding that neither the author nor the publisher is engaged in rendering counseling or therapeutic services. If such advice or other expert assistance is required, the services of a competent professional person should be sought.

This book is dedicated to my mother, Yael Kaisman, whose wisdom, love, and unconditional support are the bedrock of all that is wonderful in my life.

And to the tens of thousands of audience members and students whose enthusiasm provides the constant inspiration for our work.

INTRODUCTION

I clicked "End Meeting" on Zoom. My zombied tenth graders were done. At 4:30 p.m., I crossed the threshold from work to life: the door to my bedroom.

I'd heard my boys walk in just a few minutes before, and I was excited to give them hugs and hear about their day.

I opened the door, took a half a step, and tripped over a hoverboard. That stupid hoverboard.

Then the tornado hit.

"What's wrong with you?" I shouted from a place of rage so deep inside I didn't even know it existed. And then I proceeded to launch into a 15-minute tirade about everything you've ever heard about what-not-to-do-and-say-as-a-parent.

It was September 2020 and my anxiety was catching up with me. Those sleepless nights wondering when the virus will hit us. My calculated risks day in and out for each member of our home. Zoom school. And the fear. So much fear.

It hadn't always been this way.

I grew up privileged. Privileged in a way that is deep, meaningful, and life changing. I grew up with an abundance of emotional health and well-being with two parents who loved us, nurtured us, and taught us what it meant to be our best selves.

My parents are people who deeply own and choose the values and beliefs that guide their life and the life that they chose for us. Through the ups and many downs of my teenage years, I had the luxury of always knowing I could fall back on my incredible parents. They were my bedrock. Internal success and emotional resilience was the culture of our home.

My mom, Yael, is a noted educator, lecturer, and coach, who focuses her lectures on the contents you'll find in this book—in particular, the themes of internal success and authentic self-value. In my early adult years, I was introduced to *Mindset* by Stanford professor Carol Dweck, which fundamentally shaped the way I operated in tandem with internal success. My privilege set me up for success.

About ten years ago, as a gift to my mother, I collected her lifetime of work and concepts into a book called *The Internal Success Revolution*. I did everything I could to get that raw manuscript published. I reached out to dozens of leaders from all sorts of sources and took every daring risk I could to get someone of importance to read and hear what we had to say. A few incredible people agreed to speak with us, but ultimately, no one was interested in our manuscript. I struggled between wanting to persist and wondering when to accept the fact that our best was not enough.

The manuscript sat on my computer.

After my third son was born, I found the courage to share the raw manuscript. I paid for a basic cover design, published it on Amazon, and sold a few hundred copies over the next few years—mostly to those who attended our lectures, as well as our students and clients. Mostly, though, I lost passion for the project.

Then came the COVID-19 pandemic. More than COVID the disease, what struck me the most was COVID *parenting*. And COVID *living*. And COVID *coping*. Living in a COVID world was a whole new beast for which I found myself completely unprepared. While I usually consider myself to be resilient, confident, and self-assured, this time I completely fell apart. My parenting completely fell apart. My calm completely fell apart. I turned into someone consumed by intense anxiety day and night.

The worst part about this spiral was that *I* was disappointed and disillusioned with who I had become. Where before I had always had answers and self-assuredness, I suddenly felt uncertain and full of doubt. My parenting suffered dramatically. More than the impatience and the shouting, it was the way I felt inside that was slowly eating away at my mental health—like an insidious spread of anxiety eating away at my core.

As I spiraled down internally during COVID, I felt like I lost so much of the grounding and confidence that had been second nature to me. And, as we started to leave the acute pandemic phase, I feared that I had lost that sense of calm and resilience forever.

That's when I decided to revisit this work eight years after it was first published. In coming back to myself post-COVID—as a person, a wife, a mother, an educator—I realized that everything I needed to heal myself was in the pages of my own book. While I had never explicitly and consciously developed myself as a person of internal success, it was clearly time to start, and I began to do the hard work.

The book you now have in your hands is no longer a book written for my mother or by my mother. It combines her knowledge and experiences with a piece of *my* heart. This book helped me find my way back to myself to be the best version of myself I want to be.

I have, however, included stories throughout the book that share insights Yael has gathered through her years of working with individuals and families to build internal essence. The names and details have been changed, but these are all based on actual situations.

I hope that as you read through the book, you recognize the life-changing opportunity that is available to you, free of charge, free of judgment. I hope that you find the kind of support that helped me figure out how to let go of external validation and judgment, look inward, and ultimately be free of anxiety and self-judgment.

I hope, dear reader, that you'll discover the lifesaving mindset that this book provided for me during the most tumultuous and anxiety-ridden journey of my life.

And I hope, above all, that this book helps you become the best version of yourself and enables you to live a life far beyond your wildest dreams.

CHAPTER ONE

JUST YOUR AVERAGE SPECIAL PERSON

Welcome to Lake Wobegon, where all the women are strong, all the men are good-looking, and all the children are above average.

—Garrison Keillor

A few years ago, I decided to get a PhD. Yes, it was a lofty goal. But I was surrounded by friends who had doctorates and who were so encouraging about my chances of being accepted into the program of my dreams. I, too, started to believe it was possible. It was the best feeling in the world.

I was going to apply all the motivational beliefs and achieve my dreams.

I envisioned and manifested positive vibes of success.

I wholeheartedly gave myself over to the rigorous application process.

I let go of fears of failure and jumped in with two feet.

I stretched out of my comfort zone and met with professors, hired an editor for my essay, and reached into the depth of my soul to be my best self.

I did everything that every meme and coach encouraged of me. I knew it was going to happen because I did everything I could *and when you do everything it all works out,* right? This is what every motivational speaker and self-help book tells you: Envision success and you will succeed.

The rejection email was that much more surprising.

I didn't see it coming. It wasn't because I didn't do my best. Or because I didn't give it my all. Or because I failed to put in the maximum effort.

I didn't get in because my best just wasn't good enough for the admissions team. Period. And that's reality. No amount of self-talk, emotional support, or participation prize can change reality.

FAILING AT THIS ENDEAVOR DOESN'T MEAN I'M A FAILURE

This is a book about real life. It's not a book that will tell you that you can achieve anything you want. It's not a book about manifesting success or working hard. Sure, those are all great, important aspects of success. But this is a book about the reality in front of you. This is a book that asks the much more difficult question:

If your best is not good enough to achieve the exact outcome you want, how do you still love yourself and feel great and special?

That's a question that troubles many of us. We start out dreaming about what we'll do when we grow up. We're so sure of ourselves, our dreams, and our special talents. We may imagine that by 20, we'll have a terrific job in the field of our choice. By 30, we'll be running the organization. By 50, we'll surely have accomplished enough to leave the rat race behind and enjoy life on the beach of our choice.

A SKY FULL OF SHINING STARS

Let me take you back to an incident in fourth grade that still resonates with me. Mrs. Johnson noisily shut the blinds, turned off the lights, and asked each of us in her class to hold a small glow stick. She gave a beautiful talk about how each one of us shines like a star, and how we're all special in our own way. In the darkness, I could feel my classmates smiling from ear to ear.

To further appreciate each of us as stars, Mrs. Johnson explained that we would each write something nice about each friend on star-shaped pieces of neon paper. She'd collect our stars and make a bag for each student, containing all the nice things their classmates had said about them. We would glue our "special" stars onto a black piece of paper to take home, knowing how special we each are as individuals in the world.

We all thoughtfully completed our stars. (Looking back, I think our compliments were as deep as, "Nice friend," and "Fun to play with at recess," but it was fourth grade after all!) I remember how I felt when I received my bag full of stars. I read each one with tender loving care, and glued them to my sheet with a tenacity I rarely showed.

As soon as I came home, I hung that poster in my room—on the wall to the right side of my bed so I could stare at it for what felt like hours each night.

At that moment, I knew I was a shining star.

But here's the thing. The galaxy is filled with shining stars. When we look at the night sky, all those incredible stars shine brightly. It's almost impossible to differentiate one star from any of the others without highly sensitive equipment.

And that's the problem with being told you're a special shining star. You and the zillions of others in the galaxy.

You may have also been told you were special as you grew up. Now, as an adult, I wonder if anyone knows what special really means and how my special is different than yours?

YOU CAN'T BELIEVE YOURSELF TO SUCCESS

This confusion has followed me throughout my life. The times when I wasn't in the popular group, didn't have the most beautiful eyes, make the sports team, land the cool job, or have that wonderful best friend made me feel unsure. I was told I was special but these disappointments certainly didn't help me understand what it was exactly that made me special.

Yet, I desperately clung on to the belief that I *was* special—because I didn't know who I would be if for some reason that wasn't true.

What seemed like sure bets became anything but. I learned about the challenges of navigating life choices and the really hard work that goes into making dreams realities. I had failures and success, and then failures again.

I was often frustrated. I would try. I'd give it my all, as I was encouraged to do. Then, quickly it became clear that often "giving it my all" wasn't going to produce the results I wanted. When I worked my hardest to score well on the SATs, I was immensely disappointed at the results. When I was rejected from a program that seemed to be the map to my future, I was crushed.

So I looked for inspiring messages to motivate me.

"If you try hard enough, you can succeed at anything."

"Dream big, everything is possible."

"If you set your mind to it, you can achieve it."

It became apparent none of these things were true—I, like many others, have been fed a lifetime of lies. I realized this is a conspiracy—everyone knows this, but no one will come out and tell you.

Now it's true that hard work often did get me further than I might have expected. And in most cases, greater effort did lead to improved results. But that wasn't the case *all the time*. And if the result wasn't exactly what I wanted, I didn't actually care.

IF EVERYONE IS SPECIAL, THEN NO ONE IS

In *The Blessings of a Skinned Knee*, psychologist Wendy Mogel describes a disturbing trend. "If the pressure to be special gets too intense, children end up in the therapist's office suffering from sleep and eating disorders, chronic stomach aches, hair pulling, depression and other ailments." Mogel is a psychologist who saw many such children enter her office. She talks about a high school girl who began to question her own sense of value once she was exposed to a more realistic view of the world—one in which she realized that her smarts and talents were more ordinary than she was led to believe by her parents.[1]

The reality is that most of us aren't offered special treatment, leaving us feeling like victims of a world that doesn't value us appropriately.

Then there are those who want us to know that we aren't really special at all.

> In a jaw-dropping commencement address, Wellesley High English teacher David McCullough Jr. told graduates, "You are not special. You are not exceptional. . . . Across the country no fewer than 3.2 million seniors are graduating now from more than 37,000 high schools.

That's 37,000 valedictorians, 37,000 class presidents, 92,000 harmonizing altos. . . . 340,000 swaggering jocks. . . . 2,185,967 pairs of Uggs."[2]

Wow. Talk about bursting an illusion!

WHAT WE REALLY MEAN BY SAYING YOU'RE SPECIAL

In the 21st century, the first place to look for answers for almost anything is on Google. Curious to see whether others wondered what it means to be special, and, therefore, valuable, I went to Google.

Turns out, lots of people also wonder about this. I found a lively discussion on this topic: *There are seven billion people in the world, what makes me special?*

Here's what I imagined was going through the author's mind:

I've been told I was special. I believed it. My parents and teachers touted that idea, until it was as much a part of me as my right arm. Now, as I enter into the real world of adulthood, I'm starting to wonder if that's true. I've met lots of people more capable than me, even in areas where I was especially qualified. I've experienced lots of rejection and failure. And lots of those mantras that were promised as paths to success didn't give me the results I expected.

The post attracted a slew of mostly encouraging answers: You have a unique name. You have specific looks. Each person is different (like snowflakes, I presume). One respondent advised the poster that he is in fact ordinary and should just accept it (Hmmmm… that got me thinking).

Yet no one answered the actual question! The responses focused on being different, but is different *special*?

If Google couldn't give me an answer, surely my childhood guru could: Barney the Purple Dinosaur. One of my favorite songs from childhood was the Barney song with the line, *"Special. Special. Everyone is special. Everyone in his or her own way. . . ."*

As an adult, I went back to read the lyrics only to discover that the only explanation of special in the song is, *"You are special. You're the only one, You're the only one like you. There isn't another in the whole wide world, who can do the things you do."* [3]

Even Barney, that great arbiter of childhood truths, can only explain special as different.

AT LEAST EVERYONE HAS A SPECIAL TALENT—DON'T WE?

So tell me. Do we each actually have natural skills that are better than most others?

I've asked this question to thousands of people around the world. Most people insist that, yes, of course everyone excels at something. If they don't know what that is, they just haven't looked hard enough. As one confident member of an audience said, "It can be anything—everyone can find something." But is that true? *Does everyone excel at something?* And, if that *something* can't be seen by others, how do we know it's valuable? And what if that something is not especially valued in your culture? You might be able to move your left index finger in an impressive way, or say supercalifragilisticexpialidocious backwards faster than anyone else, but does that matter? When we say *something,* are we really saying *something* that *our particular culture* values?

Does it make sense, then, that everyone excels at something? That's highly unlikely, especially because we have to reckon with another reality called *average.* Which leaves us with the glaring question:

How can we excel at something if most of us, by definition, have *average* abilities?

Imagine this. You feel you have a "special" talent. Then you go to a convention filled with all the people who share the same talent. Would you still shine?

- Would you still feel smart as the bottom percentile of your graduating class at Georgetown?
- Would you still feel attractive after watching the Red Carpet at the Oscars?
- Would you still feel wealthy driving through Beverly Hills?
- Would you still feel successful when a coworker gets a promotion you had wanted for yourself?

We meet others who have greater talents than we do. We don't all excel at something. So then what do we mean when we say people are special?

SETTING OURSELVES UP FOR FAILURE

Today, in our desire to instill self-esteem and value into our children, we often shower them with praise. We want our kids to know that they're the most beautiful, brilliant, talented, gifted offspring to walk the planet. We preach about their abilities to stand out, excel, and accomplish all their dreams. After all, they're all very special.

Too many well-meaning people perpetuate these confusing messages, suggesting that everybody is smart, everyone is beautiful, and we are all "special." Ms. Duluth, a second grade teacher, teaches a unit each year on multiple intelligences.[4] Her goal is to help her students understand how they best learn.

To show each second-grade child that they're smart—an important value in our culture—she facilitates a class project in which each student figures out his or her "intelligence," so they feel smart in their own way. The bulletin board where these projects are displayed exclaims: *It's not IF you're smart, it's HOW you're smart.*

The project is creative, academically challenging, and emotionally developed, but what message does it send to kids? Take a student who has "musical/rhythmic" intelligence. They may be destined to take a lead in the school musical or produce YouTube videos at age ten, but is that what society means when we use the term "smart"? And what happens when we label seven-year-olds with these distinctions? How many potentially incredible musicians will miss their calling because they didn't score high on musical/rhythmic intelligence in second grade?

Then there are the participation trophies. You may have heard about youth sports teams that give every child a trophy. There's no first place—everyone wins! What message does this convey? Do kids think they have special qualities in sports because they brought home a trophy? What happens when they get into a real sports competition and find out they're not so talented after all? And why are we always so worried about competitions in which our kids are likely to lose?

Ah. Lose. We *hate* that word.

Failure has become popular in our culture. But losing still always sucks.

Say this together with me: "Who is a winner?. . . . Those who had fun!"

Be honest. Did you really believe it? Probably not. This is just another lie we've been told—and, worse yet, one we continue to tell our kids.

Is it possible for everyone to be a winner? Of course not. And why would you feel like a winner when you've lost the game, blown the job interview, or been rejected from your college of choice? Do you really feel like you're having fun then? I didn't think so.

Let me be clear. Having average abilities does not stand in the way of us being *spectacular human beings.* I promise, we will get there. By the end of chapter 6, you will fully and completely understand exactly how you are an outstanding person, even if most of your abilities may be average. Stay with me here.

THE SUPERIORITY ILLUSION

By definition, most people are average—or at the very least, towards the middle of the bell curve. But not us. We're the outliers—the ones that get it, the exceptions. Except that's not usually true. It turns out that while 50% of us are below average, most of us think we're above average.

Dozens of studies have been done on illusory superiority thinking and the patterns hold true every single time. A landmark study conducted by the University of Nebraska-Lincoln in 1977 found that 68% of faculty surveyed rated themselves in the top 25% for their educational skills, and 94% considered themselves above average.[5] Yes, 94% of teaching faculty think they are above average teachers. Imagine what annual reviews look like at the University of Nebraska-Lincoln.

Similarly, students in the MBA program at Stanford University consistently rated themselves superior to their peers. Less than 10% considered themselves below average, compared to fellow students in the MBA program.[6]

In many ways, this demographic *does* truly reflect exception, perfection, and superiority of the real "above average," and yet it solidifies the exact point it's trying to prove: Even smart MBA students struggle with the concept of average. Consider the fact that all—or at least almost all—students accepted to a Stanford University MBA program are above average for the population of MBA students as a whole. It's an extremely competitive program with acceptance rates at about 6%. So, yes, overall, these students are far above average.

Now consider the question asked in the research: *How do you rate yourself compared to your peers*—other smart, successful, accomplished, above average students? When seen through that lens, 90% felt confident enough saying that they were average or above average.

The superiority illusion is not about math, clearly, but about emotional perception. And regardless of how we feel, numbers don't lie.

SELF-ESTEEM AND THE ORIGINS OF INFLATED MESSAGES

Marci could barely contain her laughter as her patient, Susan, explained why she was at the therapist's office.

"My child is struggling," Susan shared. Aiden, her seven-year-old son, was a bit "slow" from the moment he was born. He was always slightly behind in his development milestones, but the pediatrician assured her there was nothing to worry about. While Susan noticed him struggling to play with other kids at two years old, she was sure that if she played with him, he would eventually learn how to play with others. More important, Susan shared, "It just comes down to the right mindset."

She proceeded to explain how the right mindset would move Aiden forward on a path of success. If she believed in him, he'd be able to get where he needs to go. And so, she soldiered on. Susan worked with Aiden on recognizing letters, throwing balls, and learning how to get dressed independently. She sat with him and groups of other five-year-olds in the park and spent her days shadowing him on playgrounds and at playdates.

When kindergarten rolled around, Susan made sure to apply to the most prestigious and socially supportive school available. She told the school all about Aiden's strengths and what a kind soul he was.

School was a disaster. After months of coaching, accommodations, and modifications, meetings with Susan and Aiden, and ongoing support, the school decided that Aiden should not return the following year. They suggested he attend a nearby school with a special education track in a mainstream school. Susan was a mess. Aiden was falling apart.

After months of academic struggle, Aiden had little self-esteem left. He was despondent and angry, quick to cry, and shied away from those who loved him most. Aiden constantly said, "I'm so stupid," and it was a fight each day to get him in the car to go to school.

All this made sense to Marci. She was about to offer a word of encouragement when Susan said, in a slightly exasperated tone, "And I don't understand why he has such low self-esteem, I tell him he's so smart all the time!"

Marci just shook her head and smiled.

Self-esteem is, essentially, your overall opinion of yourself, including your ability to be capable of meeting life's challenges and feeling worthy of satisfaction and happiness.

In the 1980s, self-esteem became an important buzzword in education and parenting guides. We sought to build self-esteem by showering praises, delivering inflated compliments, and minimizing competition. *All* children got awards, everyone was smart, and each child was special. We completed projects about ourselves and our own importance, feeling special at every twist and turn. Generation Y and Millennials (those born after 1985) were led to believe they were capable at excelling at anything they wanted to do. Through this, we believed, we were going to develop great self-esteem.

What went wrong? While we all saw the importance of strong self-esteem, we misunderstood it. Author Michael McQueen writes, "You can certainly give encouragement, affirm progress, and build confidence in young people. However, true self-esteem is always internally driven."[7]

THE PATH TO SELF-ESTEEM HAS BEEN A HOAX

Here's the problem: This is a total hoax. You can't just *give* people self-esteem. It's the by-product of a developed consciousness of value based on your inner essence, and internal successes driven by values and personal growth.

Stop for a moment and read that again. Self-esteem is not something you can create. It's not something you can give. It's not something you can force. It is simply a by-product of a life lived guided by internal essence.

Some of the confusion comes from programs and strategies that weren't grounded in sound research. Such strategies include heaping children with undeserved praise that's not based on accomplishment.

Think about Susan, the mother in the therapist's office showering her son with inauthentic compliments. What child would feel "smart" in a special education classroom?

We have to ground our efforts to build self-esteem in reality. You can't build self-esteem by merely reciting boosters or affirmations, and you can't gift authentic self-esteem to someone else—even your loved ones.

We build self-esteem through realistic and accurate self-appraisal, meaningful accomplishments, overcoming adversities, bouncing back from failures, assuming self-responsibility and maintaining integrity. All these build our sense of competence and self-worth.

So here's the big lie. We can't give self-esteem—we can't buy self-esteem. The only way to develop authentic self-value is by learning to develop an opinion of ourselves that is focused on our inner essence rather than the external outcomes of our effort. We'll talk about this in more detail in upcoming chapters.

You can't just give people self-esteem. It's the by-product of a developed consciousness of value based on your inner essence, and internal successes driven by values and personal growth.

WHEN REALITY DOESN'T MEET EXPECTATION

On a gloomy day in December, Brian walked into Yael's office. Brian was a software engineer with a hard-earned bachelor's degree with honors from a state school and a master's degree in engineering. He came from an underprivileged background, and as the first member of his family to earn a college degree, Brian was lauded as "the smart one" in his family and larger community. True to form, he successfully landed a job with a top-rated software company, as he expected.

But then something unexpected happened. Brian found himself constantly dissatisfied with his roles. He changed jobs on a frequent basis, moving from tech company to tech company, trying to find where he best fit. His visit to Yael was a moment of self-introspection. After the last two disappointing jobs, Brian realized something was wrong. Whatever he was seeking, he couldn't find without help.

With Yael's coaching, Brian began to understand what was behind his revolving door job experience. He believed each of his managers didn't understand just how smart and qualified he was. His bosses never seemed to appropriately appreciate him for his talents. Brian felt he deserved more bonuses, a larger salary, and the title to go with it.

Yael asked Brian to make a list of what he loved most about himself. He had no trouble writing down ideas and sharing them. They then looked for patterns and themes in the list. It wasn't hard. Almost all of the qualities Brian selected were related to his intelligence or academic achievements.

Because Brian's self-worth was so tied to these external factors, it's no wonder recognition in those areas was a priority for him. After all, if he wasn't the "smart one," then what made him special? If he fell to a mid-level role at his company, earned an average income, and remained a "cog in the wheel," as he put it, *who would he be?*

Brian had been drinking the external success Kool-Aid, so to speak. He believed what he'd been told—even when the reality was obviously different. Once he realized this was all a hoax, Brian was able to look at his career in a very different way. He might be average in the grand scheme of things, but that was perfectly fine.

WHAT IS AVERAGE ANYWAY?

By definition, average is "the result obtained by adding several quantities together and then dividing this total by the number of quantities."[8]

It's the place on the bell curve where most of us statistically fall. We're likely to have average abilities, average looks, and average intelligence. Of course, we'd like to think it's the other guy—the weaker student, the less intelligent coworker, the one who doesn't work as hard—who is average. But statistically speaking, most of you reading this book are, sorry to say, average—just like I am.

I'll bet you, like me, grew up believing you were special. But when we look at what average actually means, then it's just not possible we can all be above average!

Now you see the problem. Imagine a teacher telling a parent, "Your daughter Kelsey is a wonderfully average student." Certainly, the principal will be hearing from those parents (and so will Kelsey!).

We think average means *mediocre* or *ordinary*, and those qualities don't engender pride in most people. So how do we confront this discrepancy?

Here's what I've discovered.

We need to shift our thinking to focus on personal value that relates to our internal essence, our core values, and character development—not those physical realities that are out of our control.

But first, we need to understand how our physical realities—those "tools" we carry with us—combine with our internal essence to impact who we are. We'll dive into that in the next chapter.

 **WHAT WE'VE LEARNED**

- It's not possible to be special to everyone all the time. Some people may think you're special; other people may not.

- Average has taken on a bad connotation, but by definition, we can't all be above average. Reevaluate how you are special without comparing yourself to others.

- If you're waiting for others to recognize you as great, your self-esteem and self-worth are left in the hands of others—out of your control.

- Take ownership over your self-value by shifting your mindset to focus on nurturing and developing yourself. This allows you to identify your "specialness" in a much more authentic, meaningful way

CHAPTER TWO

WHO WE ARE— INSIDE AND OUT

"As long as I can remember, I had the feeling people were expecting something from me and waiting to see me succeed. There was the assumption I would rise to the occasion and come out on top," Brooke told me.

When she was in elementary school, students gathered around Brooke's desk to count how many words she wrote for each assignment, after which they'd let the class know that was the number to beat. They'd use her test scores as a bar to see if they did well compared to the "smart girl" in class.

Brooke shared her story.

I pretended I didn't care, but in reality, it bothered me a lot. Even worse, it confirmed my suspicions that because everyone expected this level of excellence from me, I had to deliver.

In high school, things got worse. But because I'd grown up thinking and feeling that I was put on a pedestal by my friends and family, the sense of self that I was building sat atop a very shaky and unhealthy foundation.

I identified myself by my talents. I was the artist, the singer, the smart girl, the basketball player. And because I excelled in those areas I assumed that I always had to excel. I put pressure on myself to keep up that level of excellence. I'd study two weeks in advance for tests, I'd stay up late perfecting a school project, I'd put in extra work to improve my performance on the court.

While that did end up building a great work ethic, the root of my actions was anything but positive. I was being driven by a sense of insecurity, fear of failure, and the constant voice in my head saying, 'You must not let everyone down.'

Because I had a deep fear of letting people around me down, if I ever did fail, or feel inadequate about anything, I had one unbreakable, untouchable rule: NEVER TELL ANYONE! *I convinced myself that if anyone ever found out I was unhappy, struggling in class, or unable to handle stress, they'd disapprove of me and cast me aside. Because after all, if your only identity is your talent, why would anyone want you without it?*

While that may sound absurd, if a fifteen-year-old tells that to themselves enough times, it becomes the only reality. And that's what happened. I projected smiles and happiness to my family, friends, and teachers, but on the inside I was a tangled ball of nerves, unhappiness, and insecurity. I felt like I was on a pedestal with the word FRAUD written over me in big bold letters, and one day people were going to wake up and realize that I was only an imposter. But I could never bring myself to become vulnerable with anyone and tell them how I was feeling, because then I would be going against my cardinal rule.

Things began to change in my senior year when I was introduced to the concept of internal vs. external success. I learned we shouldn't be building our self-esteem by using our external *talents, strengths, or abilities, but rather by basing our self-worth on* internal *essence, traits,* and values. *I learned that any innate talent you have is nothing more than a* gift *for you to use*—it's not who you are. *Who you really are is measured by your kindness, generosity, patience and effort.*

External successes—like winning a prize, getting an award, or getting good grades—are not the goal. Sure, achieving these feels good for a minute, but they're not, and never should be, the ultimate goal. External successes are fleeting, superficial, and often out of your control. Internal successes, on the other hand, like putting your all into a project, going out of your way to help a friend, or holding yourself back from responding out of anger or spite, are everlasting, meaningful, and always within your control. *Experiencing internal successes should be our goal in life, and it should be the measure of our self-worth.*

When I understood this, I gained clarity in my life for the very first time. Up until now, I'd truly been defining myself by my externality. I believed with all my heart that I had value because I could draw, sing, do well in school, or play basketball. When I couldn't do well in those areas, I'd beat myself up and think that I was disappointing everyone around me.

Now I started to understand that I was much more than just my gift. I was someone who was kind, generous, sensitive, and hardworking who could use my gifts to help those around me. More important, I began to realize that I needed to stop defining myself by how many games I won, or the grades I got, or how many friends I had. Focusing instead on how hard I played in each game, how much effort I put into studying for each test, and how many people I had around me that truly value me for my essence left room for me to be the most important thing in the world: imperfect.

I was able to let go of the idea of perfection and just be myself, no matter how many mistakes that meant making along the way. I was able to start becoming more vulnerable with the people around me and open up to them about how I was feeling, because I understood that my value was not with my talents, but for my internal essence and values.

Today, I'm still working hard to fully incorporate these ideas into my life. In a world where so much emphasis is put on externality, to truly live your life based on internal values and successes takes a lifetime of proactive work and courage. But as someone who has begun to change her life based on this revolutionary idea, I can say that it's profoundly rewarding, life changing, and incredibly worthwhile. I'm living my life more sure of myself and truly proud of who I'm becoming. It all stems from understanding and recognizing the importance of focusing on my internal essence.

UNDERSTANDING THE TRUTH ABOUT OUR EXTERNAL REALITIES

Like Brooke, we all have external qualities that we use to feel special, get ahead in life, and to identify ourselves and others around us.

Many of these are simple to define, easily seen by others, and measurable. Some are fairly obvious, such as our job, our looks, and how much singing talent we possess. It's clear to others where we live, what schools we attended, and to which family we belong. We can objectively measure our wealth, intelligence, material possessions, and the number of friends in our circle, and feel good about ourselves when we measure up.

We often speak about these traits, dwell on them, and they're usually top of mind. That's why we use them to rate and define ourselves. In the marketplace, they are almost the entire basis of our self-worth. Bosses, coworkers, potential mates, and friends are all looking and assessing us based on these qualities.

From the time children are young, we comment on their looks, their cute clothes, their ability to walk, climb, and perform at ballet. What gorgeous hair color! He can really carry a tune! She certainly has a brilliant memory!

As we grow older, many of us associate ourselves with the external realities within our lives, spending hours looking in the mirror, measuring our muscles, and obsessing about our weight and grades.

While we may also care about poverty in the world, being compassionate people, having good relationships, and having developed character traits, in reality, this often plays second fiddle to the energy we put into developing those external characteristics we show to the world.

Always remember: Regardless of external or internal successes and failures, you are valuable because *you are you*. Your very existence is what makes you worthy. Internal successes are the expression of that innate worthiness. It's like the light of your soul or personal expression.

Think of the precious metal silver. Silver is always valuable in its existence. But when it's polished, you get to really see the shine at its best. That's our internal successes.

External Qualities	Examples
These are our physical realities. Some we get at birth, some we expand, and some we acquire.	• Money • Looks • Intelligence • Home • Vacations • Material items • Job role

These physical realities can be either assets or challenges. They can be wonderful blessings—such as wealth—that make our lives more enjoyable by allowing for leisurely activities, acceptance into esteemed circles, and the ownership of material items. They can also be liabilities— such as learning challenges—that limit our academic achievements, hinder social relationships, and cause us to struggle financially.

Think of these as components in the toolbox we use to construct our lives. When you build a house, you need to consider what materials are available. After all, you can't build a brick house out of wood.

And that's where many of us get confused.

If we have a toolbox filled with positive qualities, we feel good. If we have some that aren't quite top grade, we don't.

Too often, we allow these external factors to define who we are and determine our self-value. If we get high grades, find a great spouse, make money, or are considered attractive, we feel valuable. If we experience social rejection, don't get a promotion, struggle with dating, or gain weight, we don't. We may be grateful for all we have, or feel limited and frustrated by what we lack.

But we can't let these external qualities define us, because they are *not* who we are. They may be important factors in our lives, but they're not what makes you or me significant. How you look at age 20 or at 50 is not your defining quality. Neither is your athletic success or academic challenges, your gorgeous wife or unemployed children, your acceptance to Yale or the foreclosure on your house.

We spend much of our lives attempting to achieve financial success. Some see money as a means to an end: others as an end in itself. Most people have a deep relationship with money, often associating their financial success or failure with their identity and feelings of self-worth.

A well-known philanthropist and community leader lost his fortune during the 2008 economic crisis. When he was wealthy, people came to him for money and advice, but once he was broke, that was no longer the case. He told his granddaughter, "I'm not sure why they stopped coming for advice. I'm broke, but my mind still works." We often treat others differently based on their external successes and failures.

We see this clearly in the rise in suicides during economic downturns. It's easy to say, "It's only money," but that cliche isn't helpful. Money *does* help us access enjoyable things. But money is just an external reality—it doesn't tell us about your value as a person.

For a long time, researchers believed that almost all suicide was linked to mental illness, including those that occurred during economic downturns. But a 2012 study suggests that financial loss can lead to suicide, in the absence of mental disorder.[9] The sense of external failure is just too much to handle when it's the core of self-worth and sense of achievement.

If you are not your job

And you are not your looks

And you are not your smarts

And you are not your clothes

And you are not your money

And you are not your car

then who are you?

Who You Really Are

Your definitive value is that you are a thinking and feeling being made up of character traits, capable of making moral choices, and able to grow and develop your character. These qualities define your essence, which is a reality over which you have absolute control. That's where your sustainable greatness lies.

INNER ESSENCE IS WHAT DEFINES US

So what makes you, you?

When I ask this question to a diverse audience, I always get silence.

Well, that's not quite true. I don't *always* get silence. At the beginning of my talk, I ask this question and I get a lot of confident answers. People tell me it's their jobs, academic achievements, family roles, physical features, and gender identities. Ultimately, audiences share that what makes them who they are is a combination of their accomplishments, successes, and choices along the way.

Then I talk about external qualities and we clearly establish that we are not our jobs or our academic successes or our relationships.

So I ask, again, what makes you, you?

And that's when I get total silence.

You are your internal essence. That's it. Period. That's the whole of you. We can't see it. We don't win awards for it. We can't always show it to others and we definitely can't hang it on the wall. Sometimes, we can't even describe it. But your internal essence is what makes you the person that's you.

Essence is that intrinsic part of you. Some call it consciousness. Some call it a soul. Some refer to it as your spirit. In *Star Wars*, they talk about the Force. Whatever phrase you choose, your essence is that part of you that is the moral character of who you are. And that's the most significant aspect of you.

Generosity, loyalty, persistence, honesty, humility, compassion, responsibility, are all essence qualities. Sickness, disability, imprisonment, infertility, and loss of material items don't need to change who I am, because these circumstances are not my essence. They may change the realities under which I live, but ultimately they don't need to redefine me.

And, as you will come to learn in this book, if we *never* undermine, ignore, overlook, or shortchange our essence, we will have truly lived our best life.

In his most recent book, *The Earned Life*, renowned executive coach Marshall Goldsmith talks about how we can maximize fulfillment and minimize regret by going against what much of what we've been taught about goal achievement in our society:

"We are living an earned life when the choices, risks, and effort we make in each moment align with an overarching purpose in our lives, regardless of the eventual outcome."

To get there, Goldsmith says there are three simple requirements: We must make our best choice supported by the facts and the clarity of our goals, we accept the risk involved, and we put out maximum effort.

However, he notes that "in many cases, the outcomes of our choices, risks, and maximal efforts are not 'fair and just.'... The reward of living an earned life is being engaged in the process of constantly earning such a life."[10]

Now these qualities are different for each of us. We have the potential for positive qualities within us, but we need to nurture them, develop them, and own them to their maximum. Of course, we're impacted by the environment into which we're born (nurture) and by our nature.

We're each different by nature. Some of us are flexible, others rigid; some of us are more social, others introverts. Some of us are very philosophical, others want nothing but facts, facts, facts.

Our environments (nurture) also vary greatly. Some of us are born into circumstances that give us more energy and time to focus on essence development. Others have to focus all their energy on just meeting basic physical needs. Some people get exposed to spiritual ideas early in life. Others have to work hard to find a spiritual realm—if they do at all. We all start at different points in life. But wherever you start, you have the ability to expand and grow.

Internal Essence	External Factors
• Effort	• Grades
• Values	• Money
• Persistence	• Homes
• Kindness	• Looks
• Patience	• Intelligence
• Generosity	• Family
• Integrity	• Career achievement

THE BIG LIE

Too often, we confuse our physical reality with our identity. No surprise—we've been drinking the Kool-Aid on this for our entire lives.

This misconception and confusion is at the core of most of our inner turmoil and inadequacies. We know people commit suicide during financial downturns. Why? Because when they lose their job, they feel like they've lost themselves.

Then there are athletes. We've seen even such superstars as Simone Biles and Naomi Osaka step back from competition because of the incredible pressure they face as the best athletes in their sport. Tiger

Woods' identity was so tied to his status as one of golf's best players that the only way back from a devastating car injury was to get back on the course again—even though he is, at best, a shadow of his former self.

If this impacts professional athletes, imagine what it does to those who are aspiring to make it big.

Take Erica, who began attending gymnastics classes when she was three years old. By middle school, gymnastics was her life—taking precedence over her social and family obligations. Everyone said she had potential as an Olympic gymnast, and they all supported her dream. As a middle schooler, Erica was at the gym at 5:00 a.m. to get in a three-hour workout before school, and then she'd head right back to the gym at 4:00 p.m..

Like most aspiring athletes, Erica compromised a lot in her life for her gymnastics aspirations. She gave up school events, clubs, trips, and so much more. She once told me how much she mentally suffered from the pressure. Her anxiety got worse in the eighth grade, and she started exhibiting destructive behaviors, like bulimia and pulling out her hair.

I was obviously concerned. I brought in Erica's parents, and we discussed how we could support her. At one point, we gently asked Erica if her dreams were worth the issues she was starting to face. Her parents, to their credit, even suggested Erica step back. She could remain a gymnast but not continue to compete at her current elite level.

Erica was horrified by the suggestion. "Who would I be without my gymnastics life?" she asked. Her parents nodded their heads in agreement.

Erica continued on course and was accepted to a university with an outstanding gymnastics team. Then one day, in her freshman year, she fell during a practice session.

That was it. That day marked the end of Erica's career, dreams, and, sadly, her identity. Although she didn't know the extent of the damage at the time, the fall led to complications, many doctor visits, and eventually surgery which made it impossible for her to ever reach Olympic competition levels.

Erica was devastated. She became depressed. At 18, she felt her life was over and she was useless.

I bumped into Erica years later and she told me that worse than the fall or the physical injury was the depression she faced for nearly a decade afterwards. She literally couldn't see an Erica that existed separate from Erica the gymnast. When the gymnast dream died, so did Erica. She endured years of suffering trying to find out who she was if she couldn't be an elite gymnast.

It took almost ten dark years to finally be able to see herself beyond her gymnastic abilities. Today, Erica coaches others on the danger of defining self-value based on external qualities, sharing her journey to help others.

"If only," she sighed, "I would have listened to your talks about external qualities and internal essence in school!"

Unfortunately, that's easier said than done.

Our jobs are an important part of our lives. We need to work to earn money and meet our basic needs. Sometimes, our jobs provide an important feeling of fulfillment. Often, they're part of our self-definition.

We spend so much time at work. We invest years getting qualifications, devote much effort to finding the right job, and spend most of our day accomplishing our work tasks. We often allow our jobs to define us. Who am I? I'm a teacher. I'm an engineer. I'm a mechanic. I'm a therapist.

For over 15 years, Jim was a doctor in private practice. He loved helping others and enjoyed the esteem that came with the title. Then he lost his medical license after a malpractice case and was no longer able to practice medicine. Jim felt depressed—he'd lost his sense of self when he lost his medical practice. Over the years, Jim was unsuccessful at building other qualifications, finding a new job, or even developing a new source of income. Jim is intelligent and has a large personal network, but years later he still tells us, "I'm a doctor." Helping sick people wasn't Jim's job—it was who he was.

Unemployment often causes people to question their personal value. During the Great Recession, CNN published an article about the impacts of unemployment. They analyzed the negative emotional impacts—such as depression—and even discussed the decline in physical health as a result of being out of a job. One unemployed Seattle man struggling to find work said, "You really, really, truly start to question who you are."

We all know how emotionally taxing it can be to be unsuccessful in looking for work, but unemployment shouldn't define a person's self-value. Sure it's frightening to be out of work, but viewing this as an external reality, not part of one's identity, can help us maintain our dignity, positivity ,and self-value in the face of such frustrating failure. On a practical level, developing generosity, by volunteering or getting involved in charitable causes, can help improve feelings of self-worth.

MAXIMIZING OUR EXTERNAL QUALITIES HELPS DEVELOP OUR ESSENCE

An external trait is not inherently productive or destructive for personal growth. What's important is the choice we make and how we empower ourselves to use what we've been given.

My friend Ramon exhibits this concept perfectly. He's really smart, very accomplished, and has achieved all the professional accolades and positions one could hope for in a lifetime. When you meet Ramon, you wouldn't know any of this. What's the first thing he'll say to you? He'll find out about what *you* do, ask about *your* abilities, and think about how he can support you, or how you can support someone else. Ramon lives for connection and contribution. Rather than using his positions for power or personal benefit, he spends all his time finding ways to help others and the world around him.

Here's the coolest part: Ramon's work goes beyond Ramon. Recently, he was working on a project to help support a medical non-profit. Ramon has been connecting lots of other smart and wealthy individuals to this non-profit to support their mission and work. One of those folks was Sean. Not only did Sean help the non-profit, he sent two other colleagues to help their cause. One of those people had a connection to a man who was eventually brought in to be an executive for the organization, where he made huge contributions to the work the foundation was doing.

Ramon could have simply lived a life in which he focused on using his amazing intelligence and great life opportunities to increase his power and profits. Instead, he asks himself, how can I use my position of power for contribution? How can I maximize the opportunities in my life to make the world a better place?

I recently taught a student who achieved As in all classes through minimal effort. While her intelligence was praised by all, I knew she really struggled in other areas, such as empathy towards those with learning challenges and being a team player when partnered with students who were academically weaker. Upon acceptance into a school full of other "A" students I reminded her that her value lies in her ability to develop those areas of essence and learn to have more patience, empathy, and acceptance of those who are intellectually different than her.

Sometimes our external qualities are not so desirable, and might even be painful.

Take Sam Berns. His physical reality unfortunately included progeria, a disease that causes premature aging. From birth, Sam's condition caused his body to deteriorate at a very rapid rate. In his TED talk, Sam shared how he used his unfortunate situation as a conduit for incredible self-development.[11] He viewed his disease as an external reality, not one that defined his inner essence. Sam also used his illness to inspire others and kept his sense of positivity—despite obvious tragic circumstances.

Throughout his short life, Sam impacted thousands of other people, while continuing to lead a happy life in spite of his health. He is a shining example of someone who never let his physical challenges interfere with his identity and self-worth.

Then there's Ariele and Trevor. Ariele was born deaf and raised by parents who focused on developing her inner essence. Ariele viewed her deafness simply as a challenging tool—just as you or I might view a challenge to cook or play basketball or wear glasses.

One day, Ariele heard her friend Amy talking about her colleague Trevor. She asked Amy to set the two of them up on a date. Thinking she wouldn't date a deaf person herself, Amy, very uncomfortably, asked Trevor if he would consider dating her deaf friend. "Well," Trevor responded, "I don't know. You haven't told me anything about her!" Today, they're a very happily married couple.

SUCCESS AND EFFORT DON'T ALWAYS GO TOGETHER

Remember my rejection from the prestigious PhD program? I'd tried my best, given it my all, but didn't get the outcome I was expecting.

I promised that this book would address the real question of self-worth: What happens when our best is not good enough for the results we want?

Here's the answer:

When we accomplish a challenging feat or create something special, we're told that we're amazing and wonderful. It certainly strokes our ego, but is that what makes us great? Or are we congratulating someone for being lucky enough to have the right external qualities available?

Often, successes that are applauded are predominantly based on the areas where we're naturally good, and don't reflect the sweat or effort we put in to succeed. When we truly work hard at something, we may not get thunderous applause, since we rarely are creating the kind of results that get people excited. This dichotomy forces us to wonder: What is our real greatness, as opposed to our good fortune? Greatness is more likely to be based on a deeper value of self-development, such as effort, persistence, patience, kindness, and other areas of essence development.

The reality is that many of us, even with the mindset of internal success, feel stuck. Bad habits are hard to break. It can take years to overturn such deep-seeded patterns and ingrained values of external importance but the results can be well worth the effort.

WEDDINGS

The joy of weddings. . . . and the nightmare of preparations. Sometimes, a couple planning a wedding almost sounds as if they're going through a personal trauma: "I don't have any energy, I'm planning a wedding!" Then you watch a happily dating couple become poster children for high anxiety and relationship turmoil. What happens? How can such a time of happiness and development in a relationship become a burdensome tragedy?

Somehow, instead of two people coming together to build a life of shared values and personal growth, the emphasis becomes on the external show—the wedding. We get caught up in colors of flowers, choice of halls, and large bills to pay. And while it's great to enhance the celebration of a marriage, a wedding should never become the focus of the relationship and certainly never outweigh the commitment to the relationship—even during engagement. When we're externally based, we're forever measuring our external presentation. And weddings are a significant moment for those presentations! Certainly, we want to use our creativity, aesthetics, and Pinterest/Instagram skills to make a beautiful event, but it's of minimal importance in comparison to what the wedding is really about.

Jonathan and Ella's wedding was the talk of the town. Both came from prestigious families who were active in their small community. There was much speculation over the costs, the venue, and, of course, the dress. The families came from very different cultural backgrounds and it was clear that they each had very different customs. In Jonathan's family, it was expected that the father would walk his children down the aisle, while in Ella's family, both parents did this. Friends speculated about how the families would resolve these differences.

A curious friend of Jonathan's family approached Ella's parents and asked, "So, what are you going to do? How are you going to make sure *your* custom gets followed at this wedding?" Ella's parents quickly explained, "Our custom is to do whatever the other side wants." This wedding was truly one in which the essence remained the focus.

On the other hand, there is no shortage of stories and reality shows that show the "Bridezilla" stereotype at work. The lives of couples and families are overturned by arguments about money, bridesmaids, and even such mundane decisions as color schemes. When external successes form the basis of a person's self-value, weddings are such an important time to build that bank of external success to ensure self-worth. But when we understand that our value is internal, we can focus on our ability to be generous, to treat our fiancé respectfully, and be mindful of others' needs. We can see a wedding for what it is meant to be: a celebration of love. The only real requirement is a loving couple in attendance.

SO, ARE WE ALL SPECIAL OR NOT?

There will almost always be someone who is more attractive, smarter, or wealthier than we are. There will always be something more we want to buy or achieve. Once we get it, we'll want more, and then more. When we realize that we are our inner essence, we can step off the treadmill and out of the rat race that, for many, has become the focus of our lives. We can navigate from a place of self-acceptance and love. When we focus only on our physical realities, we can detour to dark places quickly.

We need to understand and accept what we can and can't control, which is what we'll discuss in the next chapter.

 ## WHAT WE'VE LEARNED

- We each have two aspects of who we are: our internal selves and our external selves.

- Our internal self is made up of our character traits and personal development. Our external self is everything else in our physical realities: jobs, relationships, looks, wealth, education, social status, etc.

- When we frame our personal value around our external accomplishments and failures, we have a life that is dependent on others' perspective of us, results that are often out of our control, and self-value that is variable based on outcome.

- On the other hand, when we see ourselves as a reflection of our internal qualities, we can maintain control over our self-value and remain firmly self-loving.

- What makes us special is our ability to work on our internal essence and grow in our character development.

CHAPTER THREE

SEIZE CONTROL BY LETTING GO

To mask or not to mask? Eat out or eat in? Work in person, remote, or a hybrid combination?

More than two years after the start of the COVID-19 epidemic, we still didn't know the answers to many of these questions. Worse yet, we don't know *when* we'll know the answers. This ongoing uncertainty results in anxiety, frustration, and even head-to-head altercations between otherwise responsible adults.

Here's what a typical conversation sounded like in late 2021:

> *"Hey guys, let's go out—Wait... Should we go out?*
>
> *"If we go out, should we mask?"*
>
> *"How many of you are vaccinated?"*
>
> *"Hey, I know someone at work who is vaccinated and they still got COVID."*

"Well, someone I know was so strict on masks and never went anywhere. Then the one time they went somewhere, they got super sick with COVID and were hospitalized."

Before 2020, we couldn't even imagine this kind of conversation. Now it's part of our everyday lives. And this is just the beginning. Suddenly Daniella is freaking out that she might get sick. Maddie's upset that everybody's talking about masks again. Alaia announces that she's over it and everyone should just move on, while Ryan can only think about the time in March 2020 that his mother was deathly ill and hospitalized.

There's sheer chaos. And panic. And anxiety. And frustration. And anger. And resentment.

And it continues. Alaia's annoyed that Daniella is freaking out again. Daniella is upset that Maddie is busy questioning masks, when she's heard even masks may not even be enough to stay safe. And Ryan's frustrated that anyone is considering doing *anything* social in person, because it's still really dangerous out there.

By this point, the chance of dying from COVID—or even being hospitalized—is very low. So why all this anxiety? Because *this is a situation where no one has control.* Not the government. Not the medical establishment. Not schools. And especially not you and me.

Not having control in our daily lives frustrates us, causes major stress, and creates lots and lots of anxiety. We're OK with working hard, putting out effort, going through ups and downs. Ultimately, though, we expect the results to match our efforts. And when they don't, we're frustrated and demoralized.

Think about what happens when we're stuck in standstill traffic. Our anxiety, frustration, and even anger quickly escalate because we feel helpless. But if we turn on Google Maps or Waze, and hear *"There's an eight minute delay up ahead due to an accident—you're on the fastest route,*" we know what to expect. That little bit of information takes away the anxiety.

GOING NOWHERE FAST

Five years ago, I decided to leave my job as a teacher and use my educational expertise in another role. I spent months looking for the right position—spending days on job boards, connecting with friends, and pursuing every single lead I got. It was an incredibly frustrating experience and there were so many days when I wanted to throw in the towel.

A few times, I went through one or two rounds of interviews, after which I was ghosted by the recruiter. They didn't even find the time to send me a rejection! I felt so demoralized. Days turned into weeks, and I was four months into my job search. By this point, I'd interviewed with dozens of companies and gotten excited about more than one opportunity that resulted in a dead end.

I was so, so frustrated.

The most aggravating thing was I was doing exactly what everyone suggested I do. There wasn't a piece of advice I wasn't willing to take. I interviewed for jobs I didn't really want. I sent my resume to every single job that felt remotely possible. I continued to build skills alongside my job hunt, such as Google ed tech certification. I shared my search with everyone I knew, and I took every single coffee meeting and informational interview made available to me.

And I still didn't get a job offer.

I started to get anxious. What if I never get a job? What if no one wants to hire me? What if I never find my opportunity to shine? What if I can't find a way to contribute and make a difference? What if I never find my "thing"?

After six months of searching, I found a job that was a great fit. Well, I thought it was a great fit. I left less than a year later.

Now, imagine that at exactly this moment in time, my "Alexa for Life" would have turned on and told me, *"Don't worry, Shona. In exactly nine years and three months, you'll find the perfect position that will leave you fulfilled and joyful. In that job, you'll find ways to contribute to the community and use your expertise to shine and grow in your career."*

What a difference that would have made!

When we hit traffic, we can easily turn on the GPS, learn exactly how much time we'll be stuck, and accept the reality in front of us. Unfortunately, there isn't a navigation system for everyday life. But here's the fascinating thing: *We're not any more or any less in control of traffic when we know exactly what's going to happen.*

It's just that knowing how and when a situation will resolve creates the illusion of control. That gives us the confidence we need to manage the situation. If we know exactly how bad it's going to be, our minds reason, we can simply create an appropriate response and move forward.

A friend of mine got married at age 39 to the most wonderful, loving man. She joked that if someone had only told her, "Jill, you'll be single until 39, then you'll meet the man of your dreams and have many beautiful years together," she would have been less stressed about all those years she spent as a single woman. It's the unknown—the uncertainty, the obvious lack of control—that can drive us crazy and make us feel anxious and uncomfortable.

Why did COVID create such extreme anxiety? Because there was no app to tell us how long the delay would be and when we'll be safely out of the woods and traveling at the speed limit again.

THE MYTH OF CONTROL

So why do we get so frustrated over things that don't go the way we want? Why do we get so upset when life doesn't go the way we expect?

Our brains know we're mere mortals who can't control many things in our life, but our feelings often betray us into thinking otherwise. After all, we're inundated with messages that suggest that if we study hard, we'll get high grades. If we stay late at the office, we'll get a promotion. If we sign up for dating services, we'll find a suitable mate.

We're encouraged to push ourselves, and, indeed, we should.

We need to remember that while we can control our efforts, we can never fully control the results.

Take the case of David and Beth. When their daughter was born, anxiety became a third member of the family. In a therapy session with Yael, Beth announced, "I read all the books. I follow all the advice. But from the moment I put the baby down, I'm overcome with anxiety!"

It became clear that Beth, who likes structure and rules, was very anxious about her baby's sleep patterns. She did her best to create a nighttime regimen to help the baby sleep, but the results were obviously out of her control. There's nothing like the arrival of a newborn to remind us how little we control results!

Of course we know we can't fully control our wealth, our health, or the success of our family. We know we have minimal control over children, and absolutely none over the weather. But somehow we also believe in effort, hard work, and growth as the magic elixir to a wonderful life.

Think for a moment about what make us stressed. It might be a situation at work, our child's social acceptance, a stain on a new pair of pants, or finding the perfect dress for a friend's wedding. More often than not, these anxieties are really about our struggle to let go and accept our lack of control.

IF WE WORK HARD, GOOD THINGS WILL HAPPEN

So where does this control idea come from? Maybe it's the work-hard, get-rich story that makes Americans believe we can control our destiny. After all, we're taught that if we work hard, go to good schools, and be good people, we'll have a good life.

Or maybe it's because we hear so much about people like J.K. Rowling, whose *Harry Potter* books were rejected dozens of times before finding a publisher and becoming one of the best-selling book series in history. NBA superstar Michael Jordan was booted from his high school basketball team before going on to be, well, Michael Jordan. Steve Jobs was fired from Apple before leading the company to unparalleled success and introducing us to the world of iTunes, iPads, iPhones, and more.

These rags-to-riches stories lead us to believe that anything is possible if only we work hard enough. And we just can't get enough of these types of messages and narratives: They encourage us to stretch our possibilities and help us see we can be more than we ever imagined. And that's great. But, often they also skew our beliefs and encourage the myth of control. These successes aren't always just about hard work, as the stories highlight, but rather they result from a combination of exceptional talent, hard work, and a certain amount of luck. In reality, we remember them because they are the exceptions. The chance of this happening to any of us is extremely slim.

Maybe we just hate feeling vulnerable, so we delude ourselves into believing we can be anything we want to be. In fact, "Be All You Can Be" was the recruiting slogan for the US Army for 20 years. Sounds great. But, while those ads were running, the US Armed Forces rejected 71% of all recruits.[12] Imagine the shock those young people faced when they realized being all they could be just wouldn't cut it.

SO WHAT DO WE CONTROL?

Is life just a series of events that happens to us? Are we expected to sit back and watch our life go by with our hands tied behind our back?

NO!

We may not control the weather, our grades, our wealth, or our children, but there's one area of our lives where we are in absolute control: our ability to make conscious moral choices.

We're in absolute control of our effort, our reactions to what happens to us, and our ability to take initiative. We're in control about the patience we display, the empathy we offer, and the generosity we show. We absolutely and fully control our *internal success*.

The 90/10 principle, described by author Steven Covey, states that 10% of life is about what happens to you, while 90% of life is about *how you react*.[13] This principle aims to help people realize what they do and do not control. Often, we think most of our life is about what happens to us: what family we're born into, our socioeconomic opportunities, our race and religion. We can get confused and think these are what mark the outcomes of our life.

The 90/10 rule challenges that assumption by suggesting that it's not about the package we have in life, or the particular set of circumstances into which we were born or encounter along the way. Rather, it's how we *respond* to our circumstances that chart the course of our life.

We've all heard examples of those who grew up in privileged backgrounds, only to find themselves struggling in one way or another. We've heard similar examples of those who grew up in the most difficult of circumstances who made courageous choices and vastly improved their lives and the lives of those around you.

On a daily level, the 90/10 rule suggests that we need to reconsider where our control lies, and recognize that while we can't control what happens to us, we can always control our response to our circumstances. Delayed flights, lost jobs, and failed relationships are all difficult, but we have control over our response to those circumstances—and it is that response which makes up the map of our life. Wealth, education, promotion, are all wonderful things, yet we can choose to treat these circumstances with entitlement and snobbery, or recognize our privilege and react with generosity and inclusivity.

When we get anxious or frustrated in life, or even at life, it's often because we forget that yes, 10% of our life is what happens, but the far majority of the quality of our life is about how we respond to what life throws our way.

It's not about what happens to you. Your life really is about how you respond to what happens.

Diana was a twelfth grader who loved to play basketball. She was in her element on the basketball court. Then her coach benched her for the last two quarters of a game. Diana watched her team struggle to make baskets, fuming at her coach, and panicked as the team headed to a loss. She felt totally out of control.

Then Diana thought about her discussions with Yael and decided to proactively change her mindset.

"I thought to myself: *This is another example where I'm not in control of anything other than my reactions and efforts to grow.* I blew away the anger and anxiety, and focused instead on how I could cheer on and support my teammates. It was amazing! I got it! I had an internal success and it felt great."

When we get anxious about results, we waste energy on anxiety. Instead of taking actions to improve our internal essence, we spend too much time worrying. We have no control over whether we're accepted to school or hired for a job—so we walk around on pins and needles until we get an answer. We can't control the actions of our children—so we worry about them every time they're out of our sight. We don't control the way our bodies metabolize food—so we get anxious about what we eat.

Here's the funny thing: We respond to our lack of control by losing control of the one thing we can control—our reactions. How ironic.

We can study for the exam—but we can't control the questions that are asked. We can control our effort to network for dating—but we can't control whether or not we'll meet the right person. We can work hard to find a home that meets our needs—but we can't control whether we'll find the exact right house. We can try to eat healthy and exercise—but we can't control our health. The more we focus on what we *can* control—our effort and internal successes—the less anxiety we'll have about what we *can't* control—the results.

 Setting ourselves up for disappointment
We want to leave doors open for achievement.

We set the bar high (which is good).

We're then led to believe that every person is the master of their fate, (which isn't true).

Which leads to expectations that cause great anxiety and disappointment.

THE POWER OF ACCEPTANCE

The simple words, *This is another example where I'm not in absolute control*, let us release what we never should have thought was ours to control in the first place.

Molly called her therapist at exactly 8:10 on a Sunday morning. She was sitting on the couch by 2:00 that afternoon.

"I don't know where I went wrong," Molly began. Each time she started to talk, she burst into a fresh set of tears. Something was very wrong.

Molly explained:

My husband and I work very hard on our parenting. Without a doubt, it's been a huge source of success and pride in our lives. Each of our five children excels at school. They're good, kind people, and well liked by their friends.

Over the last couple of months, we noticed Hannah, our fifteen-year-old, was distracted and spending an unusual amount of time in her room. We tried to navigate the line between personal space and parental boundaries, but I felt like we were doing OK.

On Friday, Hannah asked if she could speak with us. We were thrilled. Having a teenage child ask you to talk feels like winning the lottery. I thought, 'Yes, we're good parents—we're good people. We've done well.'

That evening, Hannah got right to it and said, 'I met Tony online. We've been dating for three months. I'm in love. I'm pregnant with Tony's baby, and we're going to move in together. Tony has a job and can support us.'

There was silence. There was shock. I didn't even cry. I didn't know what to say. Was my normal family now a statistic? But more than anything else, I kept thinking, 'I failed. I'm a failure.' How could I have let this happen? What did I do wrong to get here?

Saturday morning, Hannah woke up and said goodbye. I don't even remember if I gave her a hug—it was all such a blur. Then she drove off with Tony. We never even met him! I didn't even know she had a boyfriend.

How did she even get pregnant? She was usually in her room doing homework. I had so, so many questions, but as my pregnant teenager drove off that Saturday morning, all I kept thinking was, 'I'm a failure.'

What did I do wrong? Where did I go wrong?! What can I do to make sure this doesn't happen to my other children?"

All Molly's therapist said was, "This is not about you."

"Huh?" said Molly, looking up, confused.

"That's right," her therapist repeated, "This is *not about you.*"

As parents, it's easy for us to imagine that we're puppeteers. When we first become parents, we don't know how to manage the strings of the marionette, so we take classes and learn how to be a puppet master. We learn the right method to move their arms and legs. Over time, we learn how to manage dances, expressions, and entire plays. If we pull the right strings and develop our puppeteering skills, our marionette will be a great performer.

In truth though, we're raising human beings, not puppets. There are no strings. There are no controls.

Parenting is the ultimate challenge of internal success. As parents, we so closely identify with the success of our children. We imagine our children mirror our competence. Their success means our parenting efforts are successful. But in reality, our children—as our teenagers remind us—are their own people. Yes, we birth them. Yes, we feed and clothe them and tend to all their needs. But then they go into their cocoon, grow their wings, and fly, fly away.

Molly continued intensive therapy throughout the next few weeks. She worked on the one thing her daughter Hannah needed: unconditional love and support, but it was excruciatingly difficult. Molly just couldn't express that kind of love, while engulfed in her personal failure and disappointment.

One day, she found the courage, showing up to Hannah's home with a gift card for maternity clothes. She told us how this came about:

Every time I thought about calling Hannah, I couldn't. Even though I knew in my mind it wasn't about me, I just couldn't accept it. Surely, I had to have done something *wrong to have a child make that choice. Surely, I was a failed parent.*

One evening, I got a call from my other daughter's teacher. She was calling to share an incident that happened with Evie at school. It seems that a group chat created for fun and games had morphed into a place for bullying. In the last week, two of the sophomore students were singled out, harassed, and incessantly bullied. Many students joined in. It turns out Evie was the only student in the grade who took proactive action against this behavior.

'I'm calling,' said the teacher, 'because you must be the most amazing mother. To have a daughter that can stand up to such force, to stand by her values—even at the risk of social backlash—is incredible. You must be doing something right.'

Molly burst out laughing. "If she only knew!"

It turns out Molly doesn't control any of her children—not Evie, not Hannah, not her three sons. Each child, raised by the same mother in the same household, has dramatically different outcomes.

This is the truth about parenting. And it's the truth about all relationships and outcomes in our life. We can't measure ourselves by the outcome of our efforts. We can only focus on our internal work and effort— always reminding ourselves that the outcome of the results is completely out of our hands.

The Serenity Prayer

Grant me the strength to accept the things I cannot change,

the courage to change the things I can,

and the wisdom to know the difference.

PLAY THE HAND YOU'RE DEALT

Poker more than any other game, perhaps, reflects the balance of control, luck, and skill that mirrors the game of life.

In her memoir, *The Biggest Bluff*, Maria Konnikova writes about learning and playing the game of poker as a journey to understand life more deeply. Konnikova embarks on a yearlong mission, coached by one of the greatest players, to delve into the complexities of poker and what she can learn about life through that experience.[14]

There are two particular passages that highlight the essential nature of life, as reflected in poker, that are worth exploring and, I think, provide an incredible analogy to the two courses we can use to chart our paths in life using the interval vs. external framework.

First, she talks about understanding our realistic parameters of control—the word "realistic" being the key word. It's easy for us to believe that we have control over most of our life. If we work hard enough, we'll have enough money. If we study well enough, we'll do well in school. If we are good parents, our children will be great. But none of these statements is really true. They are not "facts" or guaranteed outcomes in any way. They provide the illusion of control perhaps, but not actual control.

We all know people who worked hard and ran into tough luck. Alternatively, we also know plenty of people who got "lucky" without all the hard work.

Living in Palo Alto, I saw this over and over. My friend Nava, a recent Stanford University graduate, told me she thought there was actually a lot of luck at play, where people claimed it was all about effort and meritocracy. Take, for example, the idea of networks, or connections, and how much those impact people's careers and growth trajectories. On an even more basic level, consider race, gender, and nationality, as students vie for venture capital and seed money.

As Nava was expressing this frustration, I couldn't help but actually burst out laughing. "Nava," I said, "can we consider for a moment the incredible luck you had to even attend Stanford?"

While it's true that Nava may have been really smart, worked really hard, and done everything correctly to build a resume and essay that got her admitted to Stanford, the 97% of those rejected might have actually produced fairly similar efforts and results.

What's the difference between an accepted and rejected student at Stanford? Another friend who worked at the Business School admissions team shared tales about the complexity of the university acceptance process. You wouldn't believe what she said—or maybe you would. How many international royalty/diplomats are applying alongside you? How many legacy and university donors are in the candidate pool? Did you choose an essay topic that the committee liked, or did it happen to sound similar to three other candidates, by chance? Do you help improve the university's diversity score?

You could have worked exactly as hard as a fellow applicant. You could have had exactly the same scores and GPA. But luck and other factors outside your control, dictate acceptance for one of you and rejection for the other. Now consider how that acceptance decision might impact your next few years.

What do we really control?

Konnikova's mentor, Erik Seidel, at one point suggested that in retelling her poker plays, she only share what her hand was and how she played it. The outcome was beside the point. "Let's make a deal,"

Erik told her. "I don't care about the results of the hand. I don't care if you won or lost. When you're telling me about each hand, don't even say how it ended. I want you to do your best, but forget how it ended. That won't help you."

I reread that wise advice over and over.

It's like the parent who says, "it's not about the grade you get, it's about your preparation for the test." All we can do is our best. We study, we make the best decisions we can with the information we are given, we can reflect on the choices we made and why we made them, but we can't ever control the outcome.

The second important lesson of poker?

At one point, Konnikova shared a failed play with Seidel. Mid-sentence, he cut her off and chided her, saying, "Focus on the process, not the luck. Did I play correctly? Everything else is just BS in our heads." He continued to admonish Konnikova never to be the kind of player who blames the cards, or the other people at the table, or how the other team members played that day. It's all about what you do—what choices you make and understanding why you make them.

Imagine if we started thinking that way in our lives. What matters? How we play our hand. The hand we're given is out of our control. The outcome of our play: out of our control. The single most important thing is the process. What did we do with the cards we've been given?

We can lose sight of what we control, and we can blame others—two unhealthy and, more important, unhelpful concepts for our life. Or, we can look inward at our internal selves.

Erik Seidel's advice goes far beyond poker and directly speaks to the framework of a life focused on internal success.

STUDENT ANXIETY IS OUT OF CONTROL

Advanced Placement classes. Mandatory extracurricular activities. Worries about college acceptances. Teens face disturbing levels of anxiety disorders and destructive behaviors—sometimes even resorting to suicide.

Race to Nowhere is a thought-provoking documentary about academic stress and anxiety that documents the extreme stress and anxiety teenagers face today in their academic life. A student's grades often cast a long shadow for years—from college acceptances to career opportunities to wealth and luxuries. As the title implies, students are in a race to do well in class to get into a good school, in order to do well to get a good job, and, ultimately, to achieve something special.[15]

Achieving academic success and the prestige and opportunity that follow are good goals. But we need to look at our relationship with those achievements. Yes, it would be helpful if schools relieved some of the academic pressure, but much of the answer to self-destructive behavior lies in our ability to have a more realistic perspective of what we can and cannot control.

For many years, I lived in Palo Alto, California—a hotbed of anxious overachievers in the midst of Silicon Valley. Palo Alto has two of the top-rated public schools in the state (one of which is directly across the street from Stanford University). Local kids focus on college from a young age. They worry about their GPA and their extracurricular activities, then they scheme how to pad their college applications.

A few years ago, there was a cluster of teen suicides in Palo Alto. The community was stunned and searched for the right way to respond. Some suggested morning meditation options; others demanded more student counselors. But the fundamental problem at the core of this intense school culture is the total focus on external achievement. These kids have no choice but to connect their identity and value with how they rank in school—a reality that they can't fully control. In an area with so many high achievers, it's almost impossible for even a really good student to stand out.

Palo Alto teacher Ronen Habib created a positive psychology class to help students develop their internal qualities and achieve meaningful happiness. In an interview with the *Palo Alto Weekly*, he noted, "We don't assume, for example, that students will know how to solve trigonometric equations and so we teach that to them. Just as we teach them math, I think we need to teach them the skills that require emotional intelligence."[16]

IT'S NOT LIMITED TO STUDENTS

Let me introduce you to Rob, a very successful businessman. As he built his business and increased his wealth, Rob was able to get all the things on his dream list—a vacation home, a private chef, and his perfect car. Yet, every day he felt discouraged and depressed for not being smart enough, good-looking enough, or funny enough. It became clear to Yael that Rob felt out of control because he was prone to mood swings and anxiety. He felt like a failure for needing medication—despite all he'd achieved. Instead of focusing on his great business success and financial gains, Rob was frustrated by inner emotional turmoil.

Yael coached Rob to focus on personal development and internal success. That was life changing. Instead of ruminating on the mood swings and anxiety that he couldn't control, Rob changed his mindset to concentrate on internal success. Over time, he began to focus on how hard he worked to be patient with his children, the effort he put into developing more empathy for employees, and, ultimately, being more loving to himself in the face of high anxiety and bad moods. Rob now meets with Yael on a regular basis to share his internal successes. For those areas over which he has no influence, he constantly recites the mantra: *"Another example of what I can't control."*

THE ILLUSION OF CONTROL

Dr. Ellen Langer, of Harvard, conducted a study about the illusion of control.

Her researchers looked at scenarios in which individuals obviously had no control—such as a game of craps or winning the lottery—to assess participants' perception of control. The participants consistently believed they had control over the outcome of these chance events and tried to influence the results—even through nonsensical practices. Some felt in control by choosing lottery numbers based on personal significance, rather than randomly assigned numbers. Others seemed to roll the dice softer if they were hoping for a lower number.[17]

Clearly, we often delude ourselves into believing we can control the results even when we obviously cannot.

Winnie was struggling to know the right way to be supportive of her husband. Jim had recently left a job that had made him extremely unhappy, and now had no real direction for his career. As he spent months looking for a job to no avail, Jim began questioning his own self-worth. He wasn't sure he was as competent as he'd originally thought. Jim was self-defeatist when things didn't work out, and started feeling hesitant to pursue opportunities, because each failed job search built his feelings of inadequacy.

As his wife, Winnie tried to reassure Jim. She offered the usual supportive statements—encouraging him, telling him he was great, trying to connect him with leads for opportunities. But Jim didn't appreciate her help, which made Winnie frustrated. She wasn't sure what to do to be supportive during this tough time.

Yael worked with Winnie to find ways she could develop her self—the one thing she could control. It became clear that cutting expenses and being content with fewer material items would drastically reduce Jim's anxieties. By working on her essence to support her husband and live with less, Winnie focused on what she could control. The payoff was Jim felt supported, their marriage was strengthened, and, ultimately, they had less anxiety at home.

Albert Einstein told us that insanity is doing the same thing twice and expecting different results. To improve our relationship with our inner essence, we must change. Of course, that's easier said than done. It's certainly hard to change your behavior and thought patterns. But you really can change *your mindset.*

Throughout the day, when you feel anxious, keep reminding yourself, *This is another example of something we don't control.*

 WHAT WE'VE LEARNED

- The sources of our anxieties stem from our confusion about control.

- We only control our internal essence, not the outcome of our external qualities. We can put in tremendous effort and still fail. We can work our hardest and still lose.

- When we learn to differentiate between what we do control (internal essence) and what we don't (external realities), we recognize where to focus our efforts, and how to measure our successes and growth over time.

- When we see ourselves purely in the area of control (internal essence), we know our boundaries and can easily stay within them.

- When we shift to an internal focus, we retain control of our self-worth and we're able to have self-love—regardless of what others think or do, or the outcomes of our efforts.

- In our attempt to find control, we generally lose control of the only things we actually do control: our response and our behavior.

CHAPTER FOUR

EXTERNAL VS INTERNAL SUCCESS

Turning Things Inside Out

As newlyweds, my husband and I moved far from home to Palo Alto, California.

In this new town, everyone talked about startups. I learned there was more to stock than day trading on the NASDAQ, and I realized what terrible weather East Coasters tolerate for a good part of the year. I enjoyed the constant sunshine, the exciting innovations, and the trips to state parks. But, boy, did I constantly feel inadequate.

Here's why. I didn't go to a prep school, I didn't know there was an Ivy League–caliber college on the West Coast (just down the street from me), and I couldn't relate to many of the privileged life experiences of those around me.

After each conversation with a new friend, those feelings expanded. I had no clue what "code" was (Hint: It has nothing to do with spies.), and the concept of a degree in theoretical physics almost made my brain explode.

I pretended I didn't care. "Instead of winning a robotics contest, Shona, " I would say to myself, "You have great hospitality skills." But inside, I felt less-than. I questioned my intelligence all the time. In truth, it impacted my self-value.

So, I began to study with rigor. I attended community college, took remedial courses, and tried to matter. I avoided conversations about college, and felt embarrassed when someone assumed that if I was in college I was attending that local option—Stanford. My identity and self-worth were very much defined by my academic successes and failures.

After much hard work, a lot of tearful nights, and a few wonderful professors, I started to believe I really was valuable, because I was doing OK in my classes. My academic successes made me feel worthier. With each A, I started to feel more and more valuable.

As I neared the completion of my associate degree, someone suggested that I apply to the University of California at Berkeley. I said no, without giving it any thought, because it wasn't worth the risk of rejection. I'd finally found self-value—a potential rejection would be risking that confidence. I didn't get in, obviously, because I didn't even apply.

My values about my belief in myself have evolved. As I mentioned earlier, a few years later I applied to a PhD program at Stanford. I had very little chance of getting in. After all, I didn't have the academic pedigree they love. I didn't use the academic language they expect (I speak with emotion), and I wasn't connected to anyone to whom they owed a favor. However, it was an academic opportunity that spoke to my passions and chosen career, so I thought it was worth a try.

I met with faculty of the program, talked to graduate students, and took the GRE. I psyched myself that I could be the exception, I manifested and dreamed, I put out positive vibes. I pursued the application process with gusto. I knew statistically I had a small chance of acceptance, but I had nothing to lose to try.

You see, in the years between community college and my application for a PhD, I completely reformulated my recipe for self-value. Today, it's not connected to my academic failures (Spoiler: There was no happy ending—I didn't get accepted to Stanford!), the extra pounds I put on during the winter months, or the job rejection. My self-value is not based on the success or failure of this book, the intelligence of my children, or the number of friends that attend my birthday party. Today, my self-value is controlled by me alone. It's not based on what society thinks, what my community values, or what my friends have achieved. My self-worth is only based on my internal success—the moral and character growth that I achieve.

AREN'T OUR KIDS SMART?

"You're so cute and you're so smart!"

That's what I heard my husband singing to our first child. He was completely enamored and overwhelmed with love and joy. Like many new parents, he thought our son was the greatest and most amazing child ever born.

But I saw another, darker side to this external praise—something I wanted to stop before our son came to expect this kind of message.

I stormed into the room and demanded, "Well, what if he's not so smart?"

My husband was horrified! He felt an essential part of a parent's duty is to tell their kid they are smart.

"What kind of parent," he asked, "doesn't think their child is smart?"

He's not alone in feeling this way. A Columbia University survey found that 85% of American parents think it's important to tell their kids they're smart.[18]

But what happens when they meet someone who's even smarter than they are—much smarter? How will these children react?

From a young age, we're often taught to associate our self-value with definable and measurable external results. Our sense of value is marked by grades, awards, looks, and social popularity. We feel demeaned when we encounter academic challenges, social struggles, and athletic losses. Worse yet, we're often devastated when we discover we don't actually possess a certain talent—or when we realize we may not be so smart after all.

These messages are framed around the external qualities we discussed in chapter two. The problem is we have no control over these attributes. We can't change our ability to solve math problems, shoot a basketball, or play the flute. However, to be a fully developed person, we need to define our self-value solely on our *internal successes*—on things we really can control.

To be someone who has an authentic self-value, we need to redefine our relationship with success and failure, which means we need to focus on our essence, not these external qualities.

We can certainly still celebrate our external successes. The purchase of a new home, for example, is a sign of external success, but it should not become a symbol of self-worth. We can't allow these external successes to define our personal value. Self-value should be based on our moral and character development. This is internal success, and it provides the strong foundation for building our self-value.

By changing our perspective on success and failure and embracing that which we can control, we can develop authentic self-value that is completely independent of the external successes and failures we all experience.

THE EXTERNAL SUCCESS TRAP

External success and failures relate to our package of physical realities. This includes our success or struggle to earn money, look attractive, play sports, or master an instrument. Sometimes we're born with tools that create easy external success; sometimes we have to work hard to achieve it. Sometimes, in spite of great effort and our built-in tools, we fail. The key is to avoid associating our self-value with these external successes and failures.

Here's why.

> *When we develop self-value that's reflective of our external successes or failure, we allow the world to define our importance.*

If the world says intelligence is important and we're successful in that area, we feel special. If the world says wealth is important and we're unsuccessful creating a financial nest egg, we feel pathetic. If the world says sending our children to an Ivy League institution translates to success and our children get accepted in these schools, we feel exceptional.

The trouble is all of these successes or failures are framed around external tools, rather than our internal essence. None of these really equates to self-value. Furthermore, these external events don't build authentic self-worth.

Even more than that, the danger of defining ourselves by our external success can lead to destructive and toxic leadership, dysfunctional relationships, and an inability to see what's in our best interests. We can literally be blinded by our relationship with our external realities.

Mr. Felix was the Head of School for a school where I worked. Part of my role was to support a student and facilitate many conversations between teachers, parents, and students. I started to notice an odd and concerning pattern.

As Head of School, Mr. Felix would regularly attend meetings which seemed irrelevant to his role as Headmaster. He would offer suggestions that were not usually helpful, and seemed to insert himself in a way that reflected "Ten things not to do as a good leader." I wondered what prompted this behavior. After all, we were here to support students. Yet, many conversations became about me, as the supportive party, rather than remaining focused on strategies for the student.

An administrator at the school told me that Mr. Felix was not supported by the school community. Many saw him as incompetent at his job and grossly inadequate in his specific role. He had been battling resentment and anger for years, and spent most of his day in self-defense mode, protecting his role and defending his competence.

The administrator explained that whenever a consultant or outside educator was brought in to support students, Mr. Felix felt vulnerable and anxious. He worried they would recognize his weaknesses, which made him feel even more inadequate and anxious—an unhealthy vicious cycle. Instead of recognizing himself as a person in a position of power with responsibility to nurture the 400 students entrusted in his care, Mr. Felix saw himself defined by his position of power—something he needed to protect at all odds.

Instead of recognizing the internal essence that he might bring to the table, Mr. Felix focused on external success, cutting himself off from feedback, critique, and support from outside experts. He self-sabotaged regularly, and made decisions that were not in the best interest of the students in his classrooms—all in an effort to maintain what he viewed as his self-value: his role as Headmaster.

It doesn't have to be that way. What truly makes us special—what really contributes to our personal value—is what we ourselves control. Inner success offers an alternative way to approach failure and challenge. It allows for failure without falter. Each internal success an individual has is valuable. While twelve years of intense school work might seem fruitless without a college admission letter from a highly coveted school, each moment of patience is a victory—regardless of the moment before or the moment after. While being fired after 30 years at a job might feel terrible, the impact you had on those around you throughout those years is yours forever.

If only Mr. Felix could have seen that.

THE INTERNAL SUCCESS OPPORTUNITY

As a child, I loved playing house, especially the role of parent. There was one line in particular that I often repeated to my "children":

"Did you do your best?"

I'd say this to my dolls in my most serious adult voice. I wasn't overly precocious, I was simply imitating what was modeled for me. My parents would validate the joy or disappointment of external results, but, ultimately, they were asking me to focus on my inner successes. This approach was a way to ask if I'd developed my internal qualities—their mark of important success. While my parents certainly saw the value in academic success and growth, they were conveying the message that it was internal successes that mattered.

As a child, I'd roll my eyes and secretly wish they'd stop the psychological torture. Today, I understand what they were teaching me and I appreciate the message. I don't remember a single grade I got on a test. I can barely remember the reason I cried so much over forgotten homework. The failures I had in high school seem irrelevant as an adult.

Ultimately, though, it's the internal qualities I developed that remain an important and integral part of who I am today. The time I worked really hard to improve at math helped me develop a growth mindset for my future. The friendships I developed taught me how to navigate great relationships in the future. And the work ethic I put into areas of academic struggle is the bedrock of persistence and hard work in my life today. The internal qualities I developed along the way are how I now define my self-worth.

If I could do it, so can you! We all have opportunities to develop ourselves and experience internal successes—using those internal essence qualities within you that lead to moral and character development. It's the humility you show when you get accepted for a prestigious job. The generosity you show when others ask for help. The acceptance you show people who are different from you. The patience you display to others.

These areas of development, these internal successes, are what creates your true value.

Dr. Becky Kennedy, founder of the Good Inside parenting movement and author of the book, *The Good Inside*, highlights the dangers of external praise and validation as a measure of our own self-worth. Her advice to parents holds as true for us as for the children she's referencing.

"What's key to our mental health is the gap between how we feel with only internal validation, and how we feel when we receive external validation. We want the gap to be on the narrower side. We want our kids [*I'm adding: and us*] to be able to locate and trust their own internal estimation of themselves… and for external validation to be the icing on the cake rather than our kids [*I'm adding again: and us*] confidence and sense of being dependent on the input of others."[19]

INTERNAL ESSENCE ACTUALLY IMPROVES EXTERNAL SUCCESS

As it turns out, working on character development and inner essence often leads to greater external success. Think about a typical performance review. Yes, employees are rated for what they produce, but they're also measured on essence qualities. I've looked at many different employee review sheets and found qualities such as flexibility, courtesy, reliability, and promptness regularly included in the write-ups. Self-development, it turns out, doesn't only just feel great—it often lays the path for greater external success.

When you work on who you are, the person you become is a better employee, as well as a better spouse, parent, or sibling. When you understand how to put your ego aside, you become a more collaborative person—someone people want to get to know better.

When you work on your essence, you feel less afraid of failure. Failure is no longer tied to your self-esteem. You take more risks and, statistically, people who take more risks have more successful outcomes.

In his book, *Give and Take*, Wharton professor Adam Grant writes about why it's so important to develop the essence quality of giving to be successful in the workplace. He discusses the real benefits of being a giver and uses both academic research and case studies to show the impact that giving has on external success in the business world.[20]

By becoming more compassionate, we become better leaders. By being generous, thoughtful, sensitive, and, ultimately, giving, we are more likely to achieve external successes as well.

I see this in my classroom all the time. Students who become more engaged with their inner essence produce higher quality work. Those who lose focus on inner essence often struggle to complete assignments.

Lily, Evan, and Joe were all bright, capable students in my history class. They were grouped together for a group project, but nearly failed the assignment.

Why? None of them was willing to look past their external realities and notice each other's essence. They criticized each other, didn't listen, and got stuck in arguments about who was smarter or a better writer. In our review of the project, these usually successful students were very disappointed.

I asked them how they could have done better. Each pointed to the need for more empathy towards others. Of the three, Lily, in particular, worked on this aspect of her essence. She went on to have significant internal success and became the strongest project team leader the following year. Lily was certainly convinced of the benefits of internal success when her team learned they'd achieved the highest score in the class.

Yael had a client who spent over a year looking for a new job. Maria believed she was doing everything possible to achieve success in her interviews. She thought she'd put in her best effort and maximized her external qualities. As she talked to Yael, it became quite clear that the one thing Maria had *not* focused on was the loss of self in the process. Early in the interview process, after many rejections, she'd lost faith in herself and had stopped presenting herself as the worthy employee she could be. When Maria refocused on her essential value, she came across as a much more capable, confident candidate. A month later, she had two job offers.

What happened here? Rejection and external failure caused Maria to become anxious and even somewhat depressed about her self-value. This in turn impacted her external success. Once she was able to refocus herself on internal successes, Maria came across as more confident and more capable of achieving great things, and that led to more external success. Instead of focusing on job rejection, she celebrated her patience. Instead of focusing on financial failures, she appreciated her persistence. Instead of obsessively discussing her lack of employment, she focused on offering her time to help others. Maria didn't allow herself to be defined by rejection. Instead, she maintained confidence and self-value in spite of external failures. And, as a result, she landed a great position.

Now I can't guarantee you'll achieve external success, but I can tell you your chances are greater when you identify self-value with internal successes. Losing confidence, self-value, and optimism never did anyone any good! Reframing success and realizing where your true value lies is sure to improve your external successes over time.

INTERNAL SUCCESS STANDS ALONE

Because they're based on factors beyond our control, external successes are easily overturned by even a single failure. This demonstrates how vulnerable we are when we focus on external success. Internal success, on the other hand, is entirely independent of these outside variables.

Most external successes are a win-or-lose scenario. You get the job or you don't. You get the guy or you don't. You lose the weight or you don't. On an external level, there's no win if you fail to achieve your goal.

On the other hand, internal successes are successes each time—regardless of other moments of failure.

BUT DOES THIS REALLY WORK?

I taught this concept to a group of seventh grade students. I hoped if they internalized this concept at a younger age, it would become a formative part of their identity. If they could adjust their perspective on success to view inner success as important, they'd take more risks, cope better with failure, and experience less stress and anxiety around external results.

At some point during a lesson, Carlos asked, "If you believe in this, why don't you just grade us on effort and not the external product?"

Hmm. That was a great question. The reality is that no one, besides ourselves, can measure our inner successes. I've watched students get a C on a project while working hard to get along with their peers. I've seen other students get an A on an exam without much effort at all. I've heard students say they studied for hours—although some later admitted they were surfing the web a good part of the time! Only we ourselves can assess and applaud our inner successes. Ultimately, we live in an external world in which we can't escape external success, praises, and failures.

After pondering Carlos' question, I decided to try something different. I added a new column to each project rubric and asked students to assess their own internal successes during the project. They were to look at persistence, patience with classmates, generosity to those who needed help, acceptance of feedback, etc. I hoped this would remind them that even though they're graded on the external outcome, it's the internal success that should matter most to their self-worth.

The results were amazing. After the first project, students really began to think about these ideas through their group work. In a class that was particularly challenged by peer interactions, I noticed that as students made character development an emphasis, their external products improved as well. The leaders worked to learn when to be quiet; the quiet students learned to speak up. Rigid students worked to be more flexible for the team, while the group procrastinator focused on delivering their piece in a timely fashion. The team as a whole produced superior work. I was so proud of all their inner successes!

This idea worked so well, I incorporated it into parent-teacher conferences as well. We created a conference worksheet that asked students to rate their internal and external success on each subject. This process, though challenging for students, helped them reflect about their successes and failures in a meaningful way. It also gave them a deeper understanding of the discrepancies that exist in our external world.

Ravi had gotten a C in English, even while hoping for an A. He wrote that his internal effort was an 8 out of 10, and he was reminded of the successes he'd achieved. He may not have been happy with the external outcome, but he could now appreciate the areas in which he had succeeded.

Even more compelling was Seth, who rated himself as a 3 out of 10 in History, even though he received an A- in the class. That A- grade didn't allow him to feel superior anymore. I encouraged him to think about how he could grow—as opposed to congratulating himself on getting results with little effort on his part.

It was incredible to watch parents' reactions to their children! They were impressed their kids could complete this exercise, and they were excited to gain a clearer picture of who their child really was. Our conversations became more meaningful and honest, and each student was praised for their accomplishments, both internal and external. And they each developed a deeper and more authentic sense of self-worth.

Tasha was excited about the job interviews she'd just completed. However, despite her years of experience, she didn't get a single call back. She walked around for days moaning about her lack of value and qualifications because she didn't hear from potential employers.

Yael pointed out the obvious to Tasha. She had to be realistic, and to accept there was strong competition for the jobs to which she was applying . On an internal level, she suggested that Tasha take a quick look at her life and notice all the inner successes she had each day: The patience she worked on as a mother, the communication she was trying to improve with her husband, and the judgments she was trying to revise about others.

External rejection and failure impacts all of us. They affect our emotions and psychological well-being, but they don't have to define us.

When we're able to see our value as the combination of our inner successes, we can experience external failures and successes with a grain of salt and feel a much deeper sense of self-satisfaction.

COMMUNICATING FAILURES AND SUCCESS

We like external success: It feels good. When we experience it, we cling to it—focusing on our special abilities. When we win, we feel extraordinary and talented. When we get asked out, we feel special and beautiful. When we get invited to a party, we feel significant and popular.

When we fail or when we feel inadequate, that's when we focus on our essence as a means of solace. It's as if essence qualities are somehow only invoked when confronted with failure, rather than remaining the focal point during both failures and successes.

Most people do this because they can't see beyond external success and failures. So we say to others that something didn't take a lot of effort, when in reality it was an awful lot of work. That's a big mistake. "Effort" should *not* be a booby prize.

Often, this reality of uncertainty creates anxiety about the final outcome—even among highly successful people. Fear of rejection holds us back. It makes us both successful *and* anxious, and it keeps us from reaching our true potential.

Even more disturbing, when we praise people based on their external results, their personal value becomes tied to those external achievements. Research shows they shy away from accepting any risk that might challenge their self-value. "You're brilliant!" is the kind of praise that creates a fear of accepting challenges, while, "I'm so proud of the persistence you showed!" is more likely to encourage further growth.

Have you ever noticed how students at the top tend to worry about each point on a test? It's almost as if they'll lose their sense of self-worth if they don't maintain their usual high level of success, in whatever area they excel. It's great to win, but linking winning to your self-value almost always creates incredible pressure—whether overt or covert. No one can win all the time. Baseball players are enshrined in the Hall of Fame for getting hits in just one of every three at-bats. That means 2/3 of the time they're *not* succeeding.

Too often, we feel the need to compete with others around us. We'll discuss the effects of competition—as well as compliments and criticism—next.

THE POWER OF PRAISE

Noted Stanford University Professor Carol Dweck conducted a now-famous study about messages we send to children.

In her study, she divided the children into two groups and gave them a puzzle exercise to complete. The first group of children was praised for being smart; for the second group, the praise was for effort. In the next round of puzzles, the researchers explained to the kids that they had a choice: one puzzle was harder, though they were sure to learn more, while the other was easier.

Ninety percent of the students praised for effort chose the more challenging puzzle, while a majority of the kids who had been praised for their intelligence chose the easier way out.[21]

Effort—the ability to persist and push ourselves—is an essential quality for personal development.

WHAT WE'VE LEARNED

- External successes and failures are mostly out of our complete control. We can work on the process, but we cannot control the outcome.

- Internal successes are always completely within our control.

- When we focus on our internal successes, the times we stayed patient, acted with empathy, or remained persistent, then we can always see ourselves as winners.

- When we see ourselves as winners, regardless of the external outcomes, we are truly resilient as we become willing to take risks, quickly move from rejection, and more easily recover from failure.

- "What would you do if you weren't afraid"? When you always see yourself as a winner internally, you alleviate fear of failure and are willing to push yourself and grow in all areas, ultimately finding greater external success as a result of those mindsets. And regardless of what happens, you are OK inside.

CHAPTER FIVE

THE 3 Cs
Criticism, Compliments, and Competition

Recently, I spent time with a group of new parents. One father in particular, Justin, was lamenting his constant state of exhaustion since his son was born. He shared how he fell asleep during a meeting, dozed off while feeding the baby, and felt generally frustrated by his sleep-deprived state.

Justin had barely finished up his last thought when Jacob jumped in with exasperation, "You think *you're* tired? I'm way more exhausted!"

Yikes. If we didn't have enough competition in our lives before, now we're competing on sleep deprivation.

The world is a tough place full of competitive people who weaponize both compliments and criticism to sneak in under the armor of efforts to build internal success.

So much of our mental space is taken up by the three Cs: Criticisms, Compliments, and Competition.

Think about the last conversation you had. Did you refer to any of the three Cs? Especially the last one. Competition is something that seeps into so many of our interactions and relationships, it's almost second nature!

When we spend so much valuable mental energy focused on criticisms, compliments, and competitions, we waste valuable energy that could be used for positive self-development.

When we focus on internal essence, we will, inevitably, start to see dramatic changes in our relationships with criticism, compliments, and competition—freeing ourselves for more meaningful and positive relationships with the world around us.

COMPLIMENTS ARE ADDICTIVE

Compliments are to us as fish are to seals. A seal does a trick and gets a fish reward. They do the next trick and anticipate getting another fish.

We, too, wait for our reward. When we do something well, we expect recognition for that achievement, which we call a compliment. Once this happens, we hope—and even expect—to get a compliment for each and every achievement. When we receive them, we feel validated and seek out more success. When we don't get this external validation, we often feel less valued, demoralized, and really disappointed.

My friend Sarah has a son with beautiful features. She often get compliments about his looks. People will stop her in the mall or in the park to tell her, "You have such a beautiful child!"

This made Sarah really uncomfortable. "It's odd," she told me. "I know my child is beautiful, but why exactly are they complimenting me?"

I told Sarah she should tell people, "In truth, I waited in the right line in heaven!"

We all seek out external compliments, shower them on the ones we love, and feel they are a necessary part of building deep relationships.

"You look goooorgeous!"

"Your child is brilliant!"

"You're amaaaaazing! Of course you'll get the job!"

These comments may make us feel good, but they don't define our true essence or the real value of who we are.

Ironically, while we love the idea of getting compliments, we're uncomfortable when we actually receive them. When someone tells us, "You look terrific today," we respond with "Oh, I totally gained weight this week!" We're not sure how to handle compliments we don't feel we deserve, and so we even protest.

Compliments are usually related to our external presence. If our sense of self is derived from external factors, then compliments are important to that self-image and identity.

But there's more. We get hooked on the praise. We need regular compliments to boost our feelings of self-worth and significance. Admit it. There've been times when you achieved something amazing and all you wanted to do was tell someone else (often on social media). Sometimes, that feeling is pride. But it's often also for validation.

If a tree falls in a forest and no one is there, does it make a sound? If an achievement isn't shared with others, does it really count?

Now, I'm not suggesting this is simple to fix. In meaningful relationships, we could and should share successes and celebrate with others. But fishing for compliments, building our self-worth from the recognition of others, and measuring achievement in terms of others' perspectives can be a dangerous path.

*We have to stop caring what other
people think of us. How other people see
us is not what matters. How we see
ourselves is the only thing that counts
in a life in authentic self-value.*

The problem is we don't have an x-ray machine to see what's going on inside others. We can only see their external realities. Compliments are, in most cases, the focus on external successes. If we constantly focus on compliments and recognition, we'll lose the ability to focus on internal essence.

We don't control the outcomes of our external successes—or other people's compliments and validations. And therefore, when we focus on these external factors, we don't control how we feel inside.

That's a horrible way to live.

When, however, we can see ourselves as individuals with a mission of personal development, a shift occurs. We may enjoy hearing positive compliments but we don't *need* them to feel valuable and fuel our self-confidence and identity.

So what should we do? We need to think differently.

- It's nice to get complimented on the outfit I'm wearing, but I know I'm not a more valuable person because I look attractive.

- I'm glad people appreciated my cooking skills at the dinner party tonight, but that doesn't define my value.

- I felt good that my students enjoyed today's class, but that's where my natural talent lies. My real value is in the patience I developed as I disciplined Neema and Ellis.

- It felt great to be complimented for my work during the meeting. I'm glad I can be successful at my job and I'm proud of my development in collaboration skills that allowed me to get here.

- Winning was such a great feeling! I know my real value is in the risks I took and the personal growth I had along the way.

Imagine if we can say, "Wow! I'm so proud that today I remained calm despite the traffic," or, "I judged my partner favorably when she was late and didn't make a negative comment."

A few years ago, my son went through a bout of hitting other children at the babysitter's house. Each day, the babysitter told me what happened and I told him how I wished I could be proud of him, but I couldn't be because of his behavior. As we worked on his behavior, he began to ask each day, "Are you proud of me today?"

It turns out that even though it was important for my son to know my values about hitting, it was the external compliments that were driving his behavior. I didn't want him to be solely dependent on my feedback, so I sought to find a way for him to connect his personal behavior to his self-value. It didn't happen overnight, but after a while the behavior began to improve. With each improvement. I would respond to his unconscious request for a compliment by saying, "Sweetie, are you proud of your behavior today?" This provided him a way to assess himself and it also enabled him to be motivated by his own personal pride in his character development.

My friend Sean once forwarded me an email with a glowing review of a recent lecture he'd given. I responded back writing, "I'm so proud of you, not because of this article, but because I know you took personal risks, put in a lot of effort, and stayed true to your values. I'm also happy that all that hard work produced such joyous success." Now, this might seem a little cheesy, but it's true. I wanted to compliment Sean for the inner successes he achieved as a result of his hard work.

Rather than complimenting people's external realities, let's focus on cheerleading the effort and good choices they made.

CRITICISM CHALLENGES US

I'm not perfect—you're not perfect. We all know that. Yet, how we feel is a tricky thing. We know we're not perfect, we know everyone knows we're not perfect, and yet, we can feel so hurt when someone actually points out our imperfections. It's as if we're all hoping to keep our faults hidden—which is pretty funny when you think about it.

We experience criticism as feedback that diminishes our sense of success and can make us feel unappreciated. Think of criticism as the flip side of compliments. Criticism can be disappointing, but it shouldn't frame our self-worth, any more than compliments.

Like compliments, criticisms are usually externally driven. My sister criticizes my outfit. My mother-in-law criticizes my children. My husband criticizes the way I fold the laundry. My friend criticizes my paint color. These comments say: I don't like this part or choice about you. But sometimes, it feels like what they're really saying is, "We don't like *you*."

Now, not all criticism is helpful. Some of it is just plain nasty—delivered for the benefit of the sender, not to provide any constructive input to you, the receiver. But criticism itself isn't necessarily the problem. It's the *way* we communicate. More specifically, it's the way we *view and accept* feedback that can be life changing—if we let it.

This plays out in both the classroom and the office. Teachers and employers are encouraged to minimize criticism and to sugarcoat it with positive euphemisms—lest someone hear ways in which they are not amazing and perfect. While a report card or a parent conference is meant to provide thoughtful analysis and feedback, teachers are often encouraged to use gentle language, include as many compliments as possible, and use euphemisms instead of criticism.

"She has great potential," was a standard line found on all my report cards. What they meant to say was that if I stopped acting with utter disregard for the academic institution and its teachers, I might, someday, miraculously amount to something more than a "troublemaker." But they couldn't write that. If parents are basing their value and self-esteem on the successes of their precious children, then providing thoughtful and honest observable analysis about one's child could be seen as hostile.

If we're the products of our external qualities and tools, then thoughtful feedback is threatening.

My student Isabella often received feedback that felt insincere. She heard the word "potential" way too many times and told me, "I always wondered, given my behavior, if any of the teachers ever thought I actually had potential, or was that just a fake nice."

We don't want to hurt others, so we avoid criticism, rather than seeing it as a productive means of self-improvement. In reality, criticism can actually be essential for self-development—if we're open to receiving it. After all, while we may know exactly where our flaws are, we aren't usually aware of how much they impact others.

CRITICISM CAN ALSO BE VALUABLE

It never feels good to hear the ways in which we need to work and improve ourselves. But if we can get past the negative feelings, we can begin to see criticism from a place of strength, not weakness. Of course, we want the criticism to be kind, but even when it isn't, there's growth that can come from feedback.

I once applied for over 50 jobs consecutively. Some employers responded, most didn't. Some scheduled interviews, then ghosted me. Others led me all the way to the final interview stage—only to ignore my follow-up emails. In this frustrating process, I learned a really important lesson: Ask for criticism. I don't mean the type that's nasty and destructive, but the kind of feedback that truly provides an observable analysis of my skills.

"What would I need to have or to do to get this role?" is a question I ask all recruiters when given the chance. If I just sat through an uncomfortable and lengthy interview process and felt deep disappointment each time I was rejected, then the least I was going to get out of it was a judgment of where I was and what more I needed to do.

Adinah was a client of Yael who was fiercely competitive. She believed she was doing a great job of hiding her imperfection, as she received promotions at work and had a large group of loyal friends.

But when someone criticized Adinah, she'd quickly feel attacked and get defensive. She was sure the other person's perspective was wrong. As she worked through her feelings around criticism, Adinah admitted that people often said she was intimidating, judgmental, and that others found it difficult to talk with her.

However, her friends all denied this. "No way—it's their problem. They must be jealous," they told her in reassurance. Still, Adinah felt hurt by the criticism and accusations of others.

Adinah's mentor suggested, ever so gently, that sometimes she said things in a way that sounded pretentious and intimidating to others. Adinah decided it was time to check in with her close friends again. This time her body language and tone made it clear that she really was open to feedback.

"Of course. You're always like that—you wouldn't be you without it," one friend said.

"I feel like I always have to say something smart right away or you'll become disinterested and hang up the phone," another continued.

Adinah couldn't help but laugh at the difference in the responses. She realized she had to take a hard look at how she was fooling herself in her unwillingness to really know the truth.

It's like looking into a magnifying makeup mirror. You have to be willing to look through the magnifying glass to clearly see your flaws in order to have the opportunity to fix them. When we get defensive, we usually feel like people are seeing us as the flaw. We need to remember that criticism is just a way to help us focus on those things that really do need fixing.

THE NEVER-ENDING COMPETITION

Competition is at the core of most of our anxieties and inadequacies. It's the driving force behind our self-promotion and our constant worry—if only unconsciously: What do others think of us?

Remember the two new dads trying to outdo each other about sleep deprivation? We spend too much time looking around at what others are doing. How successful are others at work? How much money are others making? Are they happy in their marriage? They always seems so "together."

We spent a lot of our mental energy, then, assessing ourselves against what we see. It's a way for us to measure our own successes and failures. And we most often do it completely unconsciously.

Here's what happened to me recently. I was stuck in an airport waiting for a long-delayed flight with my four children. Three of them were happily playing on tablets and chatting with one another, so of course I knew I was an outstanding parent. Then my fourth child started to get restless. The restless turned into active exploration, then before I knew it, my entire handbag was dumped on the floor.

Let's be real. I was frustrated. And I let my son know it—right then and there—after which I felt bad. He'd been doing great, but of course the long delay was getting to him. It was getting to me too! He's too young to easily entertain himself and he's naturally very curious. I was disappointed in myself for reacting harshly to what was an understandable reaction, given the situation.

When we eventually boarded, it was quite some time until we could take off. A child in a seat near us fell into full-blown meltdown. Like epic, almost picture-perfect kicking and screaming. The father tried everything he could to rationalize and calm this little girl but she just wasn't having it. And then he also "lost it." He berated her, punished her, yelled at her, and did all the things we parents can do in those moments.

Selfishly, all I could think while this was going on was, "OK, Shona, you're not *such* a bad parent after all!"

You'll always find someone better, smarter, more successful than you. When we set up life as a competition, we're going to lose, and we don't like to lose

But when we're internally focused, comparisons are meaningless.

We have a choice. We can create a life of competition—categorizing our experiences into winning and losing. We can compete in our jobs, in our relationships, in our studies. We can look at others as a way to validate ourselves, which, more often than not, creates greater feelings of inadequacy and anxiety. Or we can separate external realities from our core value and minimize our competition and jealousy.

That's hard. Really hard to practice in reality. So here's a little trick. I remember that we can't pick and choose individual characteristics—we've got to take the whole package.

Then I ask myself: Would I pine for the beauty of that Instagram star, if I had to take her whole package of realities? Probably not. Would I crave my friend's job if I had to accept all that was part of his life? Unlikely.

When I think about external success this way, jealousy and competition dissipate. Furthermore, comparisons become silly. We're totally different people with totally different sets of prepackaged qualities and essences. What others have is totally irrelevant to our own lives and personal mission.

For a long, long time, lots of us have been asking and answering this question: What really makes us happy?

Often, we imagine that wealth, or at least material satisfaction will make us happy. And, to some extent, you're right. Having the security of food, shelter, and clothing without worrying does, according to research. For the US, it may cost $100,000 to pay for those things, though the exact amount varies by state and over time. Overall, having our needs met does mean a longer happier life.

The millions of dollars we dream about? Turns out, that won't really make us happier.

If you live in a nice house, can comfortably afford your mortgage, fill your cars with gas, take the occasional vacation, and not worry about day-to-day bills, you're probably pretty happy. But, let's say that you've been watching too much HGTV. Suddenly, you desire an amazingly renovated, gorgeous house like the one on TV.

Let's imagine in this fantasy that you actually get that house. Here's something that might surprise you. Research says, you won't actually be happier.[22]

I know, you're thinking, but Shona, that's not right. *Of course* I'll be happier. I just got my dream home! I'll have more friends over, my partner and kids and family will have more personal space and less conflict. I'll feel great about myself, and there will be lots of added benefits for my happiness.

Turns out though, that's all fantasy. Here's why that dream house, however fun it might be, will not actually make *you happier.*

The Hedonic Adaptation theory argues that, indeed, it's hard to improve your happiness. According to the theory, our relationship with material possessions and external successes only gives us a boost in happiness for a short period of time. When we buy our dream home, we are happier—but only for a short while. Ultimately, though, we return to the same level of happiness we had before we bought that house.

As part of the study, researchers looked at those who won the lottery and those who were denied promotions at work. Although the subjects' initial happiness changed from their successes or failures, they eventually returned to the baseline level.[23]

Clearly, external successes don't actually make us feel more content.

If the ability to possess more tools and external successes doesn't lead to greater happiness, what does?

Real happiness is the result of a meaningful, developed, fulfilled life. When we focus on achieving internal success, that's when we become truly happy.

TANTRUMS ARE NOT THE SOLUTION

My sons were once playing with one of those arcade machines with a big claw—you get to keep whatever you can catch with the claw. Each scored a plastic bowl full of goodies by the end of their turn. Then they opened their prizes and proceeded to swap around the candies—some getting better trades than others. If only real life was like that!

But, obviously, it's not. It's more like playing the claw machine on your own. You yank the claw in, you get the bowl that's chosen, and then you get to enjoy whatever's inside. And sometimes, you yank the claw in and you haven't scored anything, but the game's over.

Of course, you can be like the little boy who took his turn right after us. He had a screaming fit when he found his bowl full of Tootsie Rolls, which he clearly didn't like.

Let's get to the point. We have two options in life: Make the most of our package, or throw a tantrum. Swapping is not one of the options.

Katarina's first son had beautiful blue eyes that turned brown at 6 months. But her second son had eyes that stayed that wonderful shade of blue permanently. She and her husband posted pictures with the caption, "Such gorgeous blue eyes!" With each compliment from others they would smile and say, "Yes. Aren't they gorgeous!" Until one morning when her three-year-old began to cry, "Mommy, I want blue eyes, too!!"

If we constantly measure our personal value only in comparison to others, most of us will live our lives as losers. Once in a while, we may indeed be the most successful, but even then, our personal value needs to be independent of others. The fear of falling is strong and creates enormous anxiety for those at the top. So, wherever you fall on spectrum, the only real way to build self-value is to focus on inner growth, not to compete with others.

Nora was a vice president at a Fortune 500 company. She managed over 300 employees, performed well, and in general felt very confident. So Nora was surprised when she felt extremely competitive with a new colleague. She found herself constantly looking over her shoulder at what the other female VP was accomplishing, where she was getting recognition, how often she was publicly praised—even which executive meetings she was asked to join.

After a few months of obsessively tracking her new colleague, Nora told Yael, "I feel so insecure. Since this new person was hired, I'm no longer the best at my level. I'm watching her with jealousy, paying attention to what she's assigned, and imagining what her bonus will be. I thought I wasn't competitive or anxious all this time. Now I see that was because there was no one for me to compare myself!"

We constantly compare. It's human nature. It's so hard to see how we might frame our successes and failures without the light and context of others. And this has gotten exponentially worse with the rise of social media.

BAD SOCIALIZATION: SOCIAL MEDIA IS RUINING US ALL

We know it, but we don't want to admit it. Social media is fun, but it isn't good for us!

In her *Time* magazine article entitled, "Why Instagram is The Worst Social Media for Mental Health," Amanda Macmillan references over and over the concept of comparisons and competitiveness as the root of so much mental health dysfunction inherent in social media use. Macmillan writes the self-promotion of life and ideas on social media create a "compare and despair" attitude. When I look at others' posts, I must be less valuable, less adequate.[24]

Social media shows us an idealized version of others' lives. Funny thing—they all seem to be doing so much better than we are! Parents are coping so much more calmly. Friends have more money and nicer clothing then we do. No wonder we feel inadequate, unhappy, and even depressed.

Seeing others travel, hearing about their fun parties, and listening to their advice is not inherently unhealthy or dysfunctional. We do it all the time with friends and family as we build relationships. We all love sharing our photos, videos, and thoughts with those around us. What makes social media different?

In normal life, we're surrounded by community. This could be a small, medium, or large group, but it rarely comprises more than a few thousand people, and can often be as small as a few dozen. If we go through life comparing ourselves to those around us, however unhealthy that may be, we're competing with anywhere from a few dozen to a few thousand people.

But when we start scrolling on social media, we're now in competition with the *entire world*—all seven billion people. We're literally setting ourselves to be the biggest losers. It's hard enough to compete with those around us—why would we expand the competitive pool to be so wide?

Today's social media world is full of humble-bragging and self-promotion. To stand out, you need to find something so unique and special that you can meaningfully compete with a few other billion people that become part of your world in the interconnected realities of the 21st century.

How then do we navigate this seemingly never-ending cycle of comparisons and competitiveness and anxiety? We reframe. We get back to reality. We remember that as individuals our job is to use our external realities to develop our inner essence.

What other people are doing, what they're like, and what they accomplish has absolutely nothing to do with us and our mission. We can feel inspired by the accomplishments of others. But ultimately, we need to judge ourselves only against our own development.

Caution: Even when you *think* you're measuring yourself against your own abilities, you may actually be looking at an idealized version of yourself. This is still competing against everybody else. No, I'm not encouraging you to settle for mediocrity. Stretch yourself, work hard, but have an assessment that's based on your own capabilities and measure yourself against your own growth.

CONTRIBUTIVE RATHER THAN COMPETITIVE

I was out with a few girlfriends one night, when Camilla began to share her dating experiences with us. She read her texts, detailing her conversation with prospective dates, and making fun of some of their messages. Immediately, Alexis chimed in saying, "You think *those* guys are crazy, you have to hear *my* messages!" and quickly logged on to her dating profile to read us the messages in her inbox. They were competing about who received more unhealthy messages from prospective dates!

Amanda and John spent over a year looking at dozens of houses, hoping to find something that worked for their family's needs while staying within their tight budget. When they finally found an option that worked, they spent weeks haggling and working out a deal—finally closing on their first home. They were ecstatic! Although it was small, they were proud to have a home to call their own. It was a real achievement—especially given the years they had spent saving up for this purchase.

A few short months later, Amanda's friend Keisha called to say that she was also buying a home—at double the cost, and double the size—with significant help from family. At first Amanda felt competitive—feeling she had to justify her smaller house, telling Keisha how she and John had bought their house on their own without borrowing from family. Amanda had felt proud and thrilled of her new home, but suddenly, in light of her friend's purchase, she wasn't so thrilled after all.

Amanda was frustrated when she went to see Yael. She'd been on a high for weeks about her home purchase, and now she was disappointed. Her home suddenly felt small. She wondered why her parents hadn't offered to help with the down payment. She was busy downplaying Keisha's home because, "It was just a purchase by her rich parents." Yael worked with Amanda to understand the roots of her frustrations and put the internal success framework to use.

A home was important to both women—but it was not an essence for either of them. Yael helped Amanda understand what piece of this situation was related to external realities and what part to essence. Amanda quickly realized that possessions like this don't reflect your value, and each person has their own life "package." She was wasting so much anxious and resentful energy feeling frustrated by what Keisha had. The reality of her accomplishment was still present. Amanda and John had done a lot of internal and external work to be able to purchase their home. They'd worked together to accomplish the goal. They both made dramatic compromises. They thought about their values and stayed true to them in the purchase.

Rather than get caught up in the comparisons, Amanda realized she could be **contributive** rather than competitive. She had been so caught up in her own disappointment, she hadn't even checked to see how she could help Keisha move or celebrate her new home. With a whole new perspective, Amanda asked if Keisha needed any suggestions for a mover, if she could help her pack, and told her how much she would love to see the new home.

The opportunities to be contributive rather than competitive abound in daily conversations. Try an experiment. Listen to someone's story without quickly moving on to your own experiences. There's an amazing study which shows that you can listen to 400 words a minute but most people only speak 250 words a minute. This leaves us with 150 words that we can choose to focus on ourselves, or to give extra attention to the speaker.

There's a Talmudic saying, "Every craftsman hates members of their own craft." Even though people are often friends with those in their respective fields, there's a lot of competition in those relationships.

For years, I carpooled with other teachers to school each day. We often discussed those students with whom we were successful, since it made us feel good and stroked our ego. I now look back and realize there were so many missed opportunities for supportive conversations in areas where we had students who were struggling—because we felt too competitive to share information about these kids with our colleagues.

At times, even a more neutral conversation ended with a colleague saying, "Well, you're good at *that*, but my strengths are in *this*." Sometimes, that's the only way we can placate our competitive feelings. It's really hard to feel totally supportive and contributing to others if we're always measuring our tools and external success.

Changing our perspective to focus on internal essence allows us to give and receive compliments, hear meaningful critiques, and get off the treadmill of competition and comparisons.

WINNERS AND LOSERS

Alfie Kohn, an educational thought leader, writes extensively about research that supports the negative impacts of competition. He writes that competition creates winners and losers. By definition, there can't be more than one winner.

Kohn writes that competition actually hinders personal growth and more often makes us feel inadequate. Most of us lose most of the time. Even when we do win, the victory is a measure of self-worth based on other. True self-value is a belief in yourself, regardless of others.

Ultimately, Kohn writes, "Research has found that competition leads people to look outside themselves for evidence of their self-worth. Cooperativeness, on the other hand, has been linked to emotional maturity and strong personal identity."[25]

WHAT WE'VE LEARNED:

- **Compliments:** They're great, we appreciate them, but they shouldn't be the fuel to our fire. Awards, praise, and recognition are always wonderful, but they don't define who we are. We enjoy receiving them—but without them, we're just as worthy and lovable.

- **Criticism:** While it never feels good to be criticized, when our self-value is driven by internal successes, we can take that feedback with a grain of salt. Sometimes the messenger has a point we can accept, reflect upon, and use to improve our growth. Other times we may disagree. Regardless, we hold the power to see our own worthiness, and, therefore, we don't have to be defined by negative feedback.

- **Competition:** Stop caring what other people think. It's all about you. Competition with others is usually the core of most of our anxieties and inadequacies. Someone is always more successful, has more things, is smarter, or more attractive. Considering the fact that we're competing against billions of others online, we're doomed to be losers. When we measure ourselves in comparison to others, we give others the key to our self-worth. When we refocus on our role in developing our internal essence (not our external realities), what other people are doing/having/succeeding at is irrelevant to us. We're only really competing against our best selves.

CHAPTER SIX

THE PARENTING TRAP

"He's f***! Your son is just f***!"

I was beside myself when my son's teacher told me this. How could she say such a thing! My blood pressure rose. How could a responsible and competent educator even use that kind of language! My son is amazing, the best, a shining star! He's the leader of the class. He gets asked on dozens of playdates. He's already reading early.

He is many things, but he is definitely *not* F***.

That horrible four-letter word. The teacher had the gall to speak it aloud! F.I.N.E.

Then I thought, "Wait, no one ever told me I was *fine*. I was *amazing*. I was *the* leader. I was noteworthy and noticed. Isn't my son also outstanding?"

My heart started pounding. How could there be no superlatives, no hyperbole when I asked, "How is my child doing in school?"

Shona Schwartz, I then thought to myself, why do you care? You understand who your child is, you see his essential greatness, challenges, and potential. Who cares? Why does it matter what the teacher says? Am I really asking the teacher to compare him to others and express that he's standing out and being above? (I wasn't thinking who would be *below* at that particular moment, but I wanted my son to be *above* the rest.)

I *really* wanted my son to be more than fine. I *needed* him to be more than fine.

After I processed all of this in my head in about ten seconds, I turned to the teacher and asked, "So what are his strengths?"

What I really wanted to shout was don't you see how special and smart and empathetic he is? I figured if I asked for strengths, her face would light up, thinking about how much he contributes to the class.

She looked at me with a passive face and responded, "He always sits so nicely during reading time."

Wow. That was it. This Parent-Teacher conference was not going as I had thought it would.

When I got home, I felt pushed to reflect on my reaction. Why did this bother me so much? Why did I care so much to hear my kid excelled? Why did he have to be better than fine?

In the dark hours of the night, when I was sure no one could hear my thoughts, I secretly admitted: If my child is only just fine, am I failing as a parent?

PROJECTING AND REFLECTING SUCCESS ONTO OUR KIDS

So much of my own feelings of success and worthiness come from my kids. My ego is so deeply involved in the kind of person my kids will turn out to be, so hearing that they are truly spectacular—especially relative to others—matters to me. Unconsciously, I believed that if my kids are superior, then so is my parenting. And if my kids are less than that, it follows that my parenting must be less-than too.

As a mom, I feel like my life and my discussions with friends are consumed by parental anxieties. Should we attach or detach? Will sleep training cause better sleep or more psychological issues later in life? Should we have structured homes or unstructured creative time?

We are completely inundated with messages about what's right and wrong, what will make our kids great or disappointing.

And yet, parental anxiety is the norm. Here I am—a parent who is literally in the field of education and parenting—and I find myself consumed with anxiety about parenting issues. Is it bad that I let my two-year-old cry it out so I can feel rested and available in the morning? Should I make my children eat healthy food, or let their bodies guide them? Should I intervene in sibling rivalry, or is it better for them to work it out themselves?

Like all external outcomes, our kids are totally out of our control. I know, that's hard to believe. They're literally a piece of our existence and yet, the reality is the outcome of who they turn out to be is not controlled by the kind of parents we are. Obviously, in our role as parents, we seek to do the best we can.

But the outcome is out of our hands.

When we set ourselves up to feel successful (or not) based on who our kids become (or don't), we're inevitably setting ourselves up for frustration, disappointment, and anxiety.

If our parenting doesn't control the outcome, how do we raise our kids in a way that allows us to focus on internal success and teaching them to do so as well?

Let's look at this in more detail.

AVERAGE: THE WORD THAT WE SHALL NOT SAY

At some point during almost every speech I give to parents, I need to say a dirty word. A word that's worse than fine. A word that often makes the audience squirm with discomfort and makes me feel sweaty and shaky as I give the description.

Before I do this, I give a lengthy prologue in which I talk about my discomfort, as my shaking hands and sweating palms intensify in anticipation. I feel a need to justify what I'm about to say with a long qualification and, of course, to encourage any parent that feels uncomfortable to leave the room or simply close their ears and pretend I didn't say the word.

Average.

That's right. Average. I say it during almost every speech. At some point, I need to discuss this ugly, emotionally charged, and uncomfortable word. Average. The statistical reality that aligns with most of our existences.

It's one thing to hear that we're average in life compared to others. That's hard. It feels demoralizing. Reread the earlier chapters to confront those feelings.

But it's another thing altogether to hear that, for the most part, *the majority of us are raising average children.*

After all, raising average children means there's almost no hope for them to be accepted to the best and brightest colleges. It means they won't be musically or athletically gifted in a way that will garner trophies and awards we can show off to our friends. It probably means our children won't be featured in school newspapers or given any accolades at the school science fair.

Now, if you're the parent thinking, "Well, not *my* kids," keep reading.

If all this does turn out to be true, then how in the world are we supposed to raise a confident, successful child? What are we supposed to say to that child to make them feel special and momentous and loved and appreciated all the time? Good job, buddy, that was a nice, average performance?

The word average appears twice in the parenting equation: average *parents* parenting average *children*.

That mere thought sounds ridiculous to 21st-century parents. We are amazing parents! We're parents who read books and follow influencers. We listen to podcasts, and look up articles online. We follow the scripts of the best psychologists around the world and stay up-to-date on the latest research about how to make sure our little angels will be high performers who will accomplish and be all they want to be

But the truth is, we're probably still just average parents raising average kids.

Let's talk about exactly what that means.

This chapter is broken down into two parts. First, we'll reflect on the way we parent and the expectations on parents in today's world. Then, we'll look at the expectations of kids and the challenges that come with this 21st-century set of expectations and opportunity.

The first issue is near and dear to my heart.

GOOD ENOUGH PARENTING

When I became a parent, I wondered how I was going to raise an average child. Over time, I realized that it's accepting my average parenting that can often be the greatest burden to carry.

When my first son was born, I was given a gift: A calm, sweet, and happy baby. I thought, "I've got this." Nothing could have been a bigger gift than the confidence that first parenting experience gave me. I felt like I somehow knew the trick to raising kids right out of the gate.

And, from there, things continued. I had the luck of being an experienced educator and having an extremely involved husband. I felt like those strong women who have it figured out. I've got this.

Growth mindset was the bedrock of my parenting philosophy, sprinkled with an emphasis on internal success. I was going to raise mentally strong and resilient kids who were going to focus on taking risks, find joy in accepting challenges, and not get too much praise.

In the early years, it worked so seamlessly, I imagined I had cracked the code. I was a working mom during the day, encouraging my kids to challenge themselves on the playground in the afternoon, serving decent, healthy dinners, and never, ever, telling my kids they were smart.

As the children grew, I felt great. I was a successful parent! My kids were doing great; therefore, my parenting was excellent. Therefore, I was excellent.

But all that changed in September of 2020. Like the world around us, I came crashing down.

This didn't happen when the COVID-19 pandemic first hit in March 2020. No, then I was a mom on a mission. The Bay Area, one of the earliest areas of the country to implement shelter-in-place orders, was prepared, and so was I. Homeschool was quickly established in our 1,000-square-foot home with three school-age boys and a three-week-old son.

I aced that too. We had daily schedules that were consistent, kept learning on track, challenged the kids, and created joy (such as our daily bike rides and "drives to nowhere").

But on the COVID front, I was a wreck. My family in NJ was in the eye of the storm, with many sick family members, including my father and grandmother. I was constantly on edge. Like everyone around the world, my phone buzzed nonstop. Given my family's location, much of it was about deaths, especially of young people. I was terrified. And anxiety came calling.

My father thankfully recovered, but my grandmother did not. Like many others, in April 2020, she died alone on a ventilator in a NJ hospital. A Zoom funeral, a still recovering father, a fear of what was to come—my anxiety about COVID raced ahead.

But my parenting soldiered on. I was on solid footing.

Then September 2020 came around. To my greatest astonishment, I found I had turned into a shouting parent. *All the time*. I was quick with a frustrated tone at perfectly normal kid behavior. When a kid didn't want to listen, I was impatient and punitive. When kids didn't promptly fall asleep at bedtime, I felt overwhelmed. When the kids fought with each other or didn't express gratitude, I was quick to offer discipline in shouting tones.

Lots of parents felt that way post-COVID lockdown.

But the worst part? I felt horrible about myself—about what and who I had become—and yet, I still couldn't stop acting that way.

It seemed that as a result of external stressors, I had become like that shouting father on the airplane and I hated myself for it. How could I, someone who offers advice to others, shout at my kids? I knew all the research about positive discipline, best practices in growth mindset, and research in mindful parenting. And yet, I felt so crummy. If a client or friend would have walked into my home during some of those moments, I feared what they would have thought of me.

But even more than worrying about others, I felt intensely disappointed in myself. Why did I get impatient, I'd ask myself after the kids were at school and I had a quiet moment to myself. Why did I get hysterical when the kids didn't fall asleep on time, I'd ask in the evening.

Much worse, though, was the way I was deteriorating internally. I was supposed to be an amazing mom. I had this down. I had years of successful parenting under my belt. I understood the best way to raise kids. How could I be shouting? *What was wrong with me?*

As I worked through those feelings of inadequacy over the following few months, I turned to the very worst place to get parenting advice: Social media. Boy, did that make me feel inadequate!

It turned out, that on social media, people were not shouting at their kids. Instead, they were following well-honed scripts of emotional growth and spiritual development. Influencers and authors on all platforms were offering advice and perspectives that made me suddenly feel inadequate. Not just a little inadequate, but completely and totally inadequate. I had "shamed and blamed" my kids. I'd made them apologize (Should we make them apologize? Or, should we not make them apologize?). I'd been punitive and even sent them to their rooms.

As you might expect, I responded to all of this with the usual strategies we use when focused on external success. I felt competitive. I devalued. I mocked. I sulked.

And when I got uncomfortable enough, I finally worked through it.

I realized that in all my discussions about internal success, I ultimately felt like a great parent. I felt confident, my kids were thriving, and, overall, the external factors in my life were stable enough, and privileged enough, to feel good about my parenting.

It also quickly became clear that the great parenting I had done in the years in which I only had one or two children—who were young and relatively easy to parent—made me feel like a rockstar. I thought I'd cracked some code about raising amazing, resilient, sophisticated, intellectual, emotionally healthy kids.

It turns out, however, I'm just a normal parent. Average, in fact.

Some of my philosophies and methods worked really well over time with most of my kids. Others wore off as the kids got older or it became difficult for me to stay consistent. Some of my values became harder to follow through, as more personalities were added to the bunch and life got more hectic. Some did not survive external stressors and transitions.

I'm not the amazing parent I once thought I was. I sometimes shout. I show impatience. I react in a hectic moment.

Most important, I am in acceptance of being a great average parent. And now I know that's OK.

While we like to think we're exceptional, most of us, at least statistically, are not!

Once we recognize we're not especially amazing parents—then what? How do we still feel good about ourselves as parents? How do we see our growth? How can we feel validated and growth oriented?

You'll come to realize, as I have, that parenting, like everything else, is about reframing our internal and external success.

KIDS AS A REFLECTION ON US AS PARENTS

Edith stormed into Yael's office on the verge of tears. Her daughter,
Sophie, had recently been rejected by an elite university, which was
not only Edith's alma mater, but a school that the college counselor
had thought was the best fit for Sophie.

As she sat down, Edith burst into full-blown tears, slowly recounting
the previous day when they received the rejection letter. The whole
family was devastated. Sophie had spent years developing a college
resume for this exact school, taking on extracurricular projects and
studying late into the night. Now it felt like it was all for nothing.

Edith was inconsolable. Yael tried all the usual coaching tactics.
They talked about option B choices for schools that Sophie could attend, highlighted research that shows the college you attend doesn't

define your income over a lifetime, and discussed the fact that the college rejection was an external failure that was out of both Edith's and Sophie's control.

But Edith couldn't hear any of that. She was truly a mess. She kept bemoaning the time and money she'd put towards supporting Sophie during her high school years. The vision she had for Sophie's future felt like it had now vanished into thin air. Yael tried to provide tools to support Sophie through this disappointment and navigate the experience positively.

Then, in one of the most incredibly transformative parenting moments, Edith looked up and, through a face full of tears, slowed her breath, and said, "If I'm honest, I think I'm much more disappointed by this rejection than my daughter."

Whoa. This courageous mother expressed something to which many of us as parents can relate.

So much of what we want or need for our children is what we want or think we need for ourselves.

When our whole childhood and our whole life has been framed by external successes or failures, external validation, and recognition, this becomes part of our innate understanding of who we are and our self-worth. If our experience in being rejected by partners, career opportunities, or universities helps define and shape who we are internally, those focuses on external results become paramount in our years of raising kids.

How can we be successful parents if our kids don't experience the successes we intend for them to have?

This insight is at the crux of much of our parenting anxieties. Let's imagine for a moment in an idyllic world that external success and failures did not matter in parenting. No one ever shared children's grades. No one ever bragged about awards or acceptances, and no one looked at the parents of successful children with admiration and awe. If we're honest with ourselves, how much of our parental anxiety would be relieved? How much more would we be able to focus on the well-being of the children in front of us rather than the external successes that we need from our children to feed our own demons, anxieties, and disappointments?

RECOGNITION IS THE FIRST STEP

To understand parenting as a process of internal growth, we need to recognize where we're driven by our external successes and failures of our past. The first, and perhaps most important step in parenting is truly deeply understanding yourself. Sometimes that can be hard to do, but try this.

- On a piece of paper, set up a column where you write down the key external failures and successes over your life. This might include jobs, partners gotten away, or moments when you experienced financial opportunities or disappointments.

- Reflect on the list. In a second column, write down examples of how those experiences may have shaped some of your parenting methods or anxieties.

We can only bring ourselves to the table when we parent.

If we grew up financially struggling, how important is it for us to make sure our children are financially stable or well off? If we grew up with parents who were overbearing about our academic successes, how do we respond to our children academically as a result of that experience? If we had parents who didn't give us access to high-quality education or the emotional support we crave, how much is our parenting guided by reactions towards those disappointments of our youth?

This is not a criticism—it's a reality. We all do it. When we're completely guided by our external failures and successes, it's hard to reframe how we look at parenting success.

Now let's go back to that list and add another page.

- What are some external things that I want for my children?
  Write these down in the left column. Be honest about the
  college you want them to attend and the career you'd be most
  happy for them to have. Articulate the age at which you
  ideally would like to see them settle down and have children,
  and the salaries you want them to make along the way. Throw
  in a few awards and accolades along the way. Definitely be
  sure to include any talents you expect them to develop over
  the years.

- Now make another column in which you write about the
  internal successes you'd like your children to have—the
  personal development you want to see them develop over
  time. The character traits like patience, kindness, empathy,
  and gratitude you hope they develop. Wasn't the first list so
  much easier than the second?!

- Now, honestly, grade importance next to each aspiration—is
  each of these items extremely important, somewhat important,
  or not really important at all?

When we complete this activity, it's easy on a philosophical level to rate internal success high. After all, we all want our kids to be kind and empathetic and gracious and tolerant. But are we realistically rating the importance of internal vs. external qualities? In other words, if we would brag to our friends about our child's recital more than we would their improvement in kindness to their siblings, rate that accordingly.

What's fascinating is that in completing this exercise with many parents, the results are similar in almost every demographic: younger parents and older parents, various religions and races, different countries and cultures.

WHAT WE SAY VS. WHAT WE DO

I attended a parenting/student training where students in seventh and eighth grade and their parents were invited to attend a well-regarded training program focusing on student well-being and academic anxiety. The trainer began by asking the parents how they would define their children's success in the future. Unequivocally, the smart, educated, elite parents that made up the group shared that success for their children would mean happiness. In other words, as long as their children were happy, they would feel like they were successful parents and their children were successful.

Before I could even react to this moment, Mia, a clearly hostile seventh grader, sitting immediately to my right, turned to me and said, "What a bunch of liars!

I needed to learn more about this perspective.

The following day in class, we made time to discuss what the students saw and heard from their parents. Students expressed an enormous amount of frustration over the evening program. Many shared Mia's feelings that their parents pay lip service to their children's happiness and personal moral development, but, in reality, they're significantly more focused on external achievements, successes, and failures.

Mia then shared a story which shed light on her anger the previous evening. She had been struggling socially, and, as a result, started to develop mental health issues and social anxieties. Mia talked about how difficult it was for her to come to school each day and how much she struggled during recess and lunch times with her friends. Mia's parents knew about her challenges and brought her to a therapist, which showed incredible support for her mental health.

Mia shared that the previous week, she came home with a 100% grade on her math test. That grade was quite unusual both for her and that class in general, and her parents celebrated the success accordingly. They couldn't help sharing it with everyone they knew, because they were so thrilled about her achievement and accomplishment.

This enraged Mia. Each time her parents referenced that grade, shared it with others, and, especially when they taped it to the fridge, she felt incensed. She told me that in that moment, she knew that even though her parents paid lip service to her mental well-being, at the end of the day, what mattered more were her academic achievements. She saw her parents keep her struggles a secret, hiding them from others, and, even though they showed general support, she realized they didn't joyously celebrate her small improvements.

That's why Mia was furious when the parents—including hers—insisted their children's happiness was their chosen expression of success.

Mia is certainly not the only child who has seen this. Why does this happen?

There are two key reasons we give children confusing messages about what we consider successful and adequate. First, parents are incredibly subjective and intertwined with their children's growth, development, and success. Even though we theoretically know that our jobs are to guide and facilitate our kids' development.

> It's hard not to imagine our kids as extensions of ourselves and, therefore, reflections of who we are as successful and competent people.

Secondly, internal success is not widely recognized by others, which makes it a more difficult metric of achievement to measure. If the success of our children reflects on our success as parents, then external success more easily and clearly highlights that achievement and recognition—both by ourselves and others.

So first, let's talk about us. After all, when it comes to parenting, it's all about us.

Look back at the chart you created about success and failure and how you rated those moments. Hopefully, this gave you clarity about how we unconsciously focus our parenting. If we celebrate external achievements and feel devastated by external failures, our children automatically get the message that those are the moments that truly matter.

Remember our discussion about booby prizes and effort? Think about this. When was the last time you recognized your child's process and internal success when they were successful? From what I see, it's usually in moments of failure. The message then becomes clear: When you win, hooray for you! When you fail, well, we'll hopefully find something valuable about you anyway.

While we don't mean or intend to give this message, it's really what we show all the time.

Imagine for a moment that your child came home with an amazing grade. Or they brought news about becoming friends with the most popular kid at school. Or being chosen for the school musical or soccer team.

What would be your response? Would it reflect on internal essence (areas within your child's control) or on external realities (which are mostly out of their control)?

Here's an example:

"Buddy, that's awesome that you made the team! You're a star athlete and I knew you would make it! You're amazing!"

The message? You are awesome because you made the team. What makes you amazing? You've made the team. If you didn't make the team . . . welll. . . .

Let's try another one.

"It's awesome that you won the science fair! You've always been so good at science and you're so creative—you're amazing! I'm always so impressed by the way your board looks and it's amazing how you come up with such original ideas for the experiments. I'm so proud of you and we must share with grandma and grandpa."

The message? You're amazing because you're creative and great at science, and you manage to produce incredible products which others recognize.

See the problem?

INTERNAL SUCCESS IN PRACTICE

Perhaps, those are not quite the messages we intend to send.

So how can we reframe? A simple question can reshape our feedback: Are we focusing on internal essence or external realities

Creativity? An external reality.

Athleticism? The same here.

Smarts? This one too.

Persistence? Internal essence.

Collaboration? As is this.

Accepting critique? And this.

We want to recognize success, appreciate it for what it is, but always keep the spotlight on the essence—what we can control.

Think back to both examples. If you have a pen handy, highlight the external words in the first set of feedback. Now, let's try this again.

"Buddy, it's great that you got on the team—I'm sure you're thrilled. I'm really proud that throughout the summer you kept up your weight training, which was a huge commitment. I know it wasn't easy but that kind of persistence made me incredibly proud and that's what makes you amazing!"

"It's awesome that you won the science fair—it's always exciting to win something. I'm really proud of the way you worked with your friends on the project. I know at times it was hard for you to agree with ideas you didn't like, but the way you learned how to work together as a team and show kindness to others was the real win from where I'm standing. You're such a special budding scientist!"

It can be overwhelming as a parent to read these long scripts and imagine repeating them in the moment. But remember, it's not about the script. *It's about staying focused on essence instead of external physical realities.*

Whether they have a failure or a win, comment on the essence. Always keep the focus on the essence. Always celebrate the essence.

So how do we start to confront and combat this unconscious parenting route? We reflect upon our own value systems. If we're still in a place in which external success and failure are our guiding light of self-value, accomplishment, and adequacy, we will no doubt bring that message to our children. We will experience our kids as extensions of our own successes and failures as a parent, as they experience their own external successes and failures.

However, when we start to realize that our children are not extensions of us, we start to see that our job is to help facilitate and foster internal development in our kids—not simply be a shiny mirror. Every kid wants to experience external success and every human is disappointed by external failure. We don't have to teach those values. They will understand, if not explicitly then through osmosis by those around them.

Our job as parents is to respond to the externality of our world by focusing on the internal successes of our children. What does that look like?

CREATING AN INTERNAL SUCCESS HOME

Creating a home that's focused on valuing internal success must be done explicitly and consciously. While every family constructs a rhythm that works for them, here are a few places to start.

First, reflect upon the kinds of successes on which you'd like to focus as means for celebration.

My son recently won second place in his first science fair project. I was glad he won a prize and he was pretty excited, but I very carefully crafted my message to him.

I shared that it feels wonderful to win second place and I was glad he got that opportunity. Then I told him that, most important, I was proud that he had worked collaboratively with others. Even during difficult moments with his team when he wanted to give up, he remained part of the team. I highlighted that fact over and over. I emphasized that I was so proud because he stuck it out, brought his best self to the table, and was kind and respectful to everyone. That's what makes him awesome! (I do need to admit: This discussion came with a lot of eye rolling and also, a huge hug!)

When it comes to external successes and failures, first recognize and empathize with the success or failure and then highlight and engage with the internal development that came along with it.

I saw this lesson come to light for one of my 6th grade soccer athletes, Tommy. This particular school was centered around athletics and winning the sports season was the focus for many of my students.

Tommy was chosen by his soccer team to be the captain. Tommy was strong and athletic, though he had some challenges getting along with others and being a team player. However, during soccer season, he stepped into his leadership role with grace, working collaboratively with others, and thinking about what was best for the team, not just himself.

With his leadership, his team made it to the final competitions against local schools. The hype escalated as the entire middle school prepared for the competitions. In the final game of the season, Tommy's team was expected to win. It was a huge shock when they lost, 6-1. Tommy was devastated and, as a 6th grader, he simply couldn't understand how his team had lost. He kept saying over and over again, "Everyone knew we were better. Everyone knew we were going to win," and he found it hard to accept that even with their athletic talent, they lost the game.

Here's what I did in that moment. First, I empathized with his loss. We talked about disappointments and how bad they feel. We made the connection between the Super Bowl, which had just happened.

We imagined what it must have felt like for the losing team to have made it to the Super Bowl—only to leave without the win. We discussed the joy of the moment, the disappointments, the silver linings.

Most important, when we got back together as a class, I asked everyone to share one way that they thought Tommy had shown strong leadership moves. We used the opportunity to talk about leadership, and, as a class, we looked at some of the choices that Tommy had made as a leader to build a great team of soccer players. We spoke about the fact that even though wins feel good and losses are disappointing, recognizing what Tommy achieved as a leader is really an incredible win—regardless of the outcome of the game. Tommy's tears slowly turned into a smile. I remember his mom later telling me, "I thought he would be more disappointed." I just smiled inside and knew that our message had gotten through.

When kids hear messages that highlight internal growth, they start to understand very quickly where your values and their greatness lie.

But, too often, we give them the wrong values right out the gate.

Do you have a genius child who walked early? A child who has gorgeous blonde hair that gets lots of attention? A child who sings the ABCs by age two? A child who, from the moment they could speak, has confidence and poise?

Well, if you experienced any of these things—which you may have, if you're not like one of us average parents raising average kids—then you qualify as a successful parent.

Wait . . . what?! (screeching brakes here!)

When kids are young, we want them to feel great. And we want to feel great as parents. So without thinking that much about it, we do what all natural Millennial and 21st-century parents do: We look out for signs of genius and excellence, and then film them, post them, share them, and celebrate them.

It's thrilling as a parent when other parents at the park comment on the way our kids speak, or play, or just how young they can do the monkey bars. It's a great feeling when our kids write handmade birthday cards, knowing the other parents will be impressed, and when we watch others look to them as leaders on the playground.

When we can find something that seems "special" about our kids, that often makes us, usually unconsciously, feel somehow more special or more gifted or more adequate as parents, because our kids accomplished these external feats at such a young age.

Then the kids get a little older. All these external measures of our kids show up in preschool and elementary school in the form of progress reports, awards, and social popularity.

Ever watch a group of young parents talk about their kids? It's like a who-can-one-up-each-other-about-their-kid-the-most competition: My kid can already read! My kid can already do multiplication! My kid has been chosen for the elite baseball team! Of course, we're all socially acceptable and most of us never say those things out loud. But, somehow, people know these things about our special kids. More concerning: Our kids know that people know these special things about them.

And then, in the next stage of our children's growth, we see larger transitions, as they move into the preteen and teen years. Our children themselves quickly absorb these messages and start to prioritize and associate their own self value with external successes and failures. Rewards received, academic achievements, acceptances, social opportunities—even physical beauty and looks—become the basis for our teens' self-value and worth.

Well . . . that makes things seem a bit dire and hopeless.

How do we realistically mitigate these messages and communicate internal success to our children? The easiest way is to always give your children feedback that's focused on internal success or failure. In many ways, it's focusing on their personal development, as opposed to the external outcomes.

When we always keep the spotlight on who they are—not what they've done—they'll know that matters most to us. They'll start to own that this is what should matter to them.

The easiest way is to always give your children feedback that's focused on internal success or failure.

Naomi's parents were caught up in this conflict. For the last two years, Naomi was struggling, socially and academically. She was slower than her peers to catch onto the alphabet. At recess, she was often chosen last for games or easily felt victim to bigger kids. She expressed, as well as a four-year-old can, feeling overwhelmed from school each day. The teachers regularly spoke with Naomi's parents about holding her back to repeat a year—only to err on the side of moving her up as summer came.

Now it was pre-K. Naomi was still struggling with her letters when everyone else had moved on to three-letter words. She was socially struggling to keep up. Again, Naomi's parents found themselves at the table asking, should Naomi repeat the year? They called me in for support.

Naomi's mother was worried about what it meant to repeat a grade. Won't she be embarrassed? Won't she feel stupid? Won't she feel inadequate and hurt for years to come? I explained that many children, especially ones who bordered the age deadline, repeated preschool years, and many were far superior and happier after they were held back and had time to develop along with their peers. I showed data about the youngest in the grade and even referenced Malcom Gladwell's *Outliers* claims about birthday and achievement.[26] I thought I'd made a pretty convincing argument.

As we wrapped up the meeting, I looked at the parents and said, "Think about what's best for Naomi. Do you imagine she might feel more comfortable and even confident having the opportunity to repeat pre-K and enter elementary school more mature and prepared?"

Naomi's father didn't miss a beat. He looked at me and said, "But what will we tell our friends?"

When we start to parent through the internal/external lens, it helps us reframe those feelings of inadequacy and anxiety. Our children's personalities, academic abilities, intellectual capabilities, talents, and looks are all things with which they were born that have no reflection on who we are. They're not in any way an extension of who we are as people.

Even when our children need support that we can provide—from tutors to therapists—the outcomes of those efforts are completely outside our control.

The only part of parenting and raising children that reflects who we are is our *response* to who our children are. I haven't yet heard about the "You're a great average parent award" just yet, but when it comes on the red carpet, I hope someone nominates me.

Being a great average parent means realizing that as average parents raising average kids, external validation is not a tool in the game we're playing. Our kids may not be singled out. We'll have our patient moments and our impatient moments. Our kids will find a mix of successes and failures—so will we. Ultimately, raising our children is a process—an often difficult and imperfect one, where lots of mistakes are made, graces are given, and growth happens in small, but hopefully consistent metrics.

The only part of parenting and raising children that reflects who we are is our response to who our children are.

When we find our essence, let go of the outcomes of our efforts, and reframe our parenting journey around our essence qualities, we then stand a chance to build a solid foundation of self-love and confidence in our kids in the few short years we have to influence them.

Ultimately, when we recognize and give value to our great average parenting of great average children, we set ourselves and our children up for a life of happiness, resilience, and authentic self-value.

My grandmother, a well-known therapist, used to say, "As long as we're doing most of it right most of the time, we're doing OK."

We're not picture perfect. We're not quote worthy and social media envy worthy. When we stop comparing, stop competing, stop focusing on external success of ourselves and others, we can start our authentic journey of meaningful parenting.

Ultimately, when we focus on internal success, we will recognize and accept our role as great average parents to wonderful average children.

THE GOOD ENOUGH PARENT

I love that phrase, that movement, that research. When I first came across the good enough parent, it was simply as a meme, but the phrase stuck with me. "Good enough" felt like a term that rejected the "winning at parenting" or "perfection parenting" of the world we live in as Millennial parents.

Most of the parenting advice I've heard made me feel inadequate, anxious, and disappointed in myself. It seemed, according to all the contemporary articles I read, that there was a secret sauce out there offering me words of wisdom, which would redeem me of any parenting inadequacies and help my children be the full and perfect humans they were meant to be.

And as I read article after article, my children still had tantrums, they didn't listen to the "1,2,3, you're out" rule, and I had too many "Is that *your* kid?" stares from other parents in the park.

Then, I started to notice another pattern of advice. Parenting is hard. Expressions of validation littered the articles and memes of the Perfection Parenting Universe. It communicates something like, "Parenting is hard, really, really hard. But if you just listen to this advice, you will feel amazing and raise resilient children who will attend top rated colleges. All your friends will compliment you as they watch your amazing child excel."

It didn't actually say that, but it also kind of did.

Along came the Good Enough Parent and I was, yep, check, that's me. This is what I strive for now.

The Good Enough Parent was originally coined by Donald Winnicott, and used in a variety of venues. In the 1980s book, *A Good Enough Parent,* Bruno Bettelheim writes, "In order to raise a child well one ought not to try to be a perfect parent, as much as one should not expect one's child to be, or to become, a perfect individual."[27]

WHAT WE'VE LEARNED

- Parenting is an exercise in recognizing where our real control lies: our internal development.

- Alleviating parental anxiety is about accepting the fact that we don't control the outcome of our kids. We control the process—not the product. We can try to help them be their best selves, to nurture them, and teach them our values, but even if we did an outstanding job, they're not puppets and they'll live the lives they choose for themselves.

- The superiority illusion is strong in parents: we all think we have exceptional kids. Remembering the rule of average and recognizing kids' specialness for their internal development will help kids be resilient and learn to see their own value through the lens of internal success.

- Good Enough Parenting and Great Average Parents are mottos we need to remember.

CHAPTER SEVEN

APPLYING WHAT WE'VE LEARNED

Do or do not. There is no try.

—Yoda

I said this book was for the strivers. For the perfectionists. For the successful ones.

The goal was to reframe our understanding of our success. To find our true self-value and own our self-love. Not to be a down-in-the-dumps study of your life.

What do all strivers, perfectionists, and successful people have in common? They're willing to do the hard work. And to stick with it. And they get rewarded by watching the magic happen.

Reading a book about ideas that reshape your way of thinking about yourself is helpful.

Engaging with a book about ideas that reshape your way of thinking about yourself is even more helpful.

But practicing ideas from a book that reshapes the way you think about yourself? That's what separates the readers from the students. The aspirational ones from the achievers. The dreamers from the doers.

The late Maya Angelou said it perfectly, "Do the best you can until you know better. Then when you know better, do better."

Now you know better.

THE CHALLENGE OF MEASURING INTERNAL SUCCESS

You've seen those magazines that fawn over people in power. Lists of billionaires, 30-under-30, and Most Successful Women fill the covers of weekly tabloids. There don't, however, seem to be lists for "Most Persistent" or "Most Improved Character Flaw." After all, that would be nearly impossible: Who can truly measure an individual's internal success?

The elementary school I attended put a strong focus on helping students build character. A "Character Award" was given at each graduation. But even in an environment that valued inner success, it was darn near impossible to measure another person's inner growth. The award usually went to someone who was naturally kind. It had to be this way—no one can measure our internal successes but us.

It's unlikely we'll ever see public praise for developing your internal essence. That may be tough truth to swallow in a world where we share our thoughts and pictures with the world on a moment's basis. (Can you imagine what Instagram posts would look like if they were limited to internal successes? Keep imagining, because the chances of seeing those posts in real life are about zero.)

When we go on ten interviews but don't get an offer, we focus on the rejection—the failure to have attained the jobs, the promotions, or the college acceptance. (Of course, those around us will politely smile and praise our effort!) And, of course, people will praise us and give awards for many of our external accomplishments. They'll celebrate us for important research, prestigious jobs, and even intelligent children. No one will ask how much effort we put into an external success. It's up to us to develop that internal meter of our real successes, and to allow that to be the root of our self-value.

HOW TO IDENTIFY INTERNAL SUCCESS

External success is easy to recognize. It's where we keep our binoculars focused most of the day. It's much more challenging to notice, acknowledge, and applaud ourselves for internal successes. Yes, it might feel strange to pat ourselves on the back. But it's important that we identify and actually acknowledge our inner successes along the way.

The first step in improving our relationship with internal success is to be able to identify, and more important, differentiate it from external success. This is an often unnatural process that requires meaningful reflection and practice to achieve.

SELF-REFLECTION: QUESTIONS TO ASK YOURSELF TO HELP IDENTIFY EXTERNAL VS. INTERNAL SUCCESS

I've put together a few questions that you can use to improve your focus on inner success. These steps will help you develop the thought process to clearly identify and differentiate between external and internal success.

- Is this success or failure related to an internal or external quality?

    Take a look at the list of external and internal qualities on page 33. In which column does this success or failure lie?

- Is this success or failure recognized by others or mostly by myself?

    Are others applauding me? Is this something I would post to the public or perhaps share with a close friend?

- Is this success or failure an important step in my mission of personal character/moral development?

    Does this directly impact the development of my personal growth or is it unrelated?

Remember Lily, the student who worked hard on her internal essence? When she finally achieved an A on a project,, she was ecstatic. As we celebrated, we reviewed these three questions.

What Lily noticed was that in addition to her A (an obvious external success), she'd achieved much more meaningful and challenging internal successes along the way. She now saw that as she'd worked on the project, she had learned to accept critique, manage her anxiety in a healthy way, and began to seek out support when needed. Reviewing these questions helped Lily differentiate external and internal success without losing focus on meaningful growth.

Another student of mine, David, struggled academically and almost didn't graduate from high school. After graduation, he decided to enroll in a community college program to become a legal stenographer. He was highly motivated, worked hard, and excelled in his new environment. It was a brand-new experience to shine in a school setting. David's friends congratulated him about his success and his ability to rise to the top of his class. Having been a student of mine for some time, David wondered if this was an internal or external success. So I asked him each of the questions above.

David realized his success was actually related to both external and internal qualities. He put in a more significant amount of effort and persistence, yet he also felt he had been given the gift of great memory retention. His effort and persistence were clearly related to his essence. This was a significant achievement from which he learned how to be persistent—surely an essential quality that will enable him to persist in his moral development.

David's external success also gives him the opportunity to develop gratitude and maximize his accomplishment for internal essence. Not all successes are clearly external or internal, they're often a combination of both.

SELF-TALK: THE INNER SUCCESS LANGUAGE

Trying to integrate this new concept without language is like being given a destination without a map to get there. The most critical way to develop an internal success mindset is being sensitive to language. We're used to celebrating victories and feeling depressed about failures, but we're rarely introspective and mindful of the kind of success we experience. Like learning a new language, this will take lots of practice and patience, but becoming proficient at the language of internal success will help us articulate and understand these ideas more clearly.

LANGUAGE TO HELP DEVELOP AN INTERNAL SUCCESS MINDSET

What kind of failure did I have?

ANSWER: External Failure

> *For those times when I put in effort, I should applaud my efforts and remember that results are out of my control. I should be loving to myself and accepting of the limitation of my tools. I will keep trying to continue to expand myself.*

For those times that I didn't put in much effort, I have to take responsibility and recognize that while I may have some limitations, it's my responsibility to expand my abilities.

ANSWER: Internal Failure

Remember that each failure is independent of any success you had in the past or will have in the future. Don't get stuck! There will always be opportunities where your essence is challenged. See these as opportunities for growth. Put in what you can to plan a winning strategy for the future and focus on what you can control to improve your essence.

What kind of success did I have?

ANSWER: External success

Where I put in effort, I should congratulate myself for the hard work. I should also feel grateful that my effort produced such great results.

For successes where I put in little or no effort, I should feel blessed and appreciative for the success that I get to enjoy, but acknowledge that much of this is based on luck and my natural gifts.

ANSWER: Internal success

I can wholeheartedly celebrate! I've accomplished something that is mine forever.

Emily was the kind of student that always graduated at the top of her class. She had the gift of intelligence—the basis of her self-value—and she always worked very hard. Like many students I meet, Emily was both very successful and extremely anxious and stressed out. Everyone always saw her as the smart one—which just made her life more stressful. On the first day of class, a friend even jokingly noted that Emily was likely to be valedictorian at graduation. And, in fact, she was.

In going through the practice steps outlined here, Emily realized that being valedictorian was only an external success. She became aware that she was experiencing internal failure at the same time. Instead of working on developing flexibility, learning to let go of control, managing her anxiety, and finding a self-value beyond her smarts, Emily achieved external success mostly because she was lucky, and all this came at the expense of her authentic personal value. Once she started seeing things from this perspective, Emily was able to appreciate the gifts she'd been given, realizing she still had really important work ahead of her.

Joel was very successful in his career, though not as successful in his home life (the reason he found a chair in Yael's office). It became clear that Joel struggled to see the value of inner essence, which undermined his inner achievement. After all, he told Yael, he worked hard, therefore he was successful.

In September, Joel decided it was time to start looking for a new job. While he liked his company, he wanted to develop more skills elsewhere, so he casually began reaching out to his network. Within two weeks, Joel landed a job at a prestigious company that offered incredible growth opportunities in his field. When Joel shared his great news, Yael used this as an opportunity to practice identifying and differentiating between internal and external failures and successes.

Using these questions, after much analysis, Joel shyly admitted (perhaps to himself!) that his new job was actually the result of a close friendship with a vice president at the firm. He slowly learned to be grateful for his successes, but to also be honest about the extent of his efforts. He began to see the real valuable successes of essence development and growth.

Natalie was a nursing student studying for her boards. She was an average student and spent hundreds of hours in preparation—a level of effort she'd never put in before and it still took her three attempts to pass. The passing mark was celebrated by her family and her friends, but they weren't aware of the roller coaster of emotions Natalie had been through. She felt like a failure when she didn't pass on the first two tries, and then felt terrific when she aced it the third time.

The most significant aspect of this experience for Natalie was learning she needed to develop more patience in reading questions and completing practice tests. Ultimately, the diligence that helped her pass the exam would lead her to be more tolerant in her interactions with other people, such as patients she would work with at the hospital. It was easy for Natalie to define herself by failing or succeeding at her exams, but the real success was that patience muscle she developed.

Bella was having a hard time finding someone she wanted to marry. In her late thirties, this became a focal point in her life. With each rejection, she began to feel more depressed. Eventually, she started isolating in her home. She refused dates, didn't check her online profiles, and began to feel negative about men.

Eventually, Bella sought out a therapist and began to re-emerge from her depression. Her new energy for life was reflected in her openness to date and the renewed effort she put into the process. She started asking people to set her up, relaxed her standards about the educational background of her dates, and kept working to be a more developed person.

Sounds like a good plan, right? Well, despite all that, Bella didn't find the right partner. Yes, she was frustrated about the process and unsure if she was doing the right thing. She questioned her self-value, but she kept focusing on internal success. Bella quickly identified this as external failure, and created a new way of thinking:

"For situations where I put in effort, I should applaud my efforts and remember that results are out of my control. I should be loving to myself and accepting of the limitation of my physical realities. I'll keep trying to expand myself."

Bella realized she'd experienced real and meaningful internal success, and found herself smiling proudly as she repeated her mantra.

Let's face it. It's easy to get caught up in external successes and failures. That's why we need to change the language of our responses to failure and success, and shift our mindset to view the importance of personal and moral development.

CHANGING YOUR RESPONSE TO EXTERNAL SUCCESS AND FAILURE

- Validate your feelings: the pain, the joy, the discomfort, the praise.

    "I don't like it. I'm disappointed. It's not what I want." Say it loudly!

- Acknowledge the effort you put into the success or failure.

    Be honest. What kind of work did you really put in to this? If you put in effort, applaud yourself. If you could have done more, recognize your responsibility to do better in the future.

- Remind yourself which aspects were out of your control.

    Ultimately, effort doesn't definitively control results. Of course, you weren't in control, unless you've become God for a day!

- Put it in perspective.

    Often successes and failures are relatively short-lived moments. The feelings of joy or inadequacy pass quickly. Ask yourself: How much will this matter in a month or a year? Of course, some realities do matter for longer. In those cases, refer to the step above.

- Laugh. Realize the absurdity of the beliefs guiding these feelings.

  Really. Laugh out loud! Voice those feelings about those external realities that now define you. Say to the mirror, "I'm now a less valuable person because I didn't get the promotion at work," and then laugh again. "I'm now a special person because the girl I liked gave me her number." Then laugh again. Maybe twice.

My friend Sherrie is a passionate poet who lost a competition. Not only did she not win, she lost to another competitor who'd already won two other times. She called me crying. "I know about the language of internal success, and I know I tried my hardest, but this is just too upsetting!"

I asked her, " If you'd won, it would have been great. But would you be a more valuable person in this moment? Does losing make you less valuable?"

Sherrie laughed and said, "Of course, my value didn't change, but I just love winning!"

We agreed that winning is more exciting but it doesn't change Sherrie's real value. Despite the devastating loss, in that moment she experienced unbelievable internal success by not allowing this loss to define her—despite her intense disappointment.

Alaia is an engineer who was recently hired at a top-rated technology company. When we met for coffee, she proudly said, "I didn't flake! I made a commitment to see you and I did it!"

Alaia's comment is a great example of how to measure your self-worth based on internal success. Sure, she'd just gotten a prestigious job, but it was her success in personal development that made her feel proud. Alaia realized reliability was ultimately a greater success for her than any specific job role, because it was an internal quality which would ultimately impact her identity and character growth.

Furthermore, Alaia viewed her job as luck, explaining to me that she often found there was little she could do to get those great jobs. She saw each job as a temporary reality that wasn't that meaningful. On the other hand, working on being reliable was a challenging inner essence goal for her and that success was hers to own forever.

Just as Alaia shared this victory with me, it's important that we each have our own partners to share our successes and our failures. Practicing the process and language of inner success is key to changing our behaviors and thought patterns. A practice partner often provides much needed perspective, as we change our relationship with external successes and failure to focus on our special personal character qualities.

STEPS FOR CHANGE: PRACTICE WITH A PARTNER

Not sure if you had an external or internal success or failure? Work with your partner to identify it using the steps on pgs 133-134.

- Use your practice partner as a listening ear—someone who can validate your feelings.

- Walk through the five steps on pgs 139-140 to change your relationship with external failures. It's important to practice these guidelines to change our way of thinking.

- Practice new language out loud to your practice partner:
  "I'm excited about our new home. I hope I can use it to further my mission of person growth."

> *You can even get more specific: "I'm excited about our new home, and to use it as a tool to grow into a more generous and giving person by hosting others in need."*
>
> *"I feel really sad about our fertility issues. I'm trying to work on not feeling inadequate and developing my ability to accept the challenge. I'm even trying to be happy for others rather than jealous of their pregnancies."*
>
> *"I'm proud of my success. I handed in all my applications on time, and I'm really improving in being less of a procrastinator."*

While it may seem silly at first, voicing such language is an important step in teaching our inner voices a new way to think and process successes and failures.

Celebrate success with your partner! Go out for drinks, buy tickets to that football game, have a night on the town! Each time you achieve success, recognize it and congratulate yourself.

Sometimes, following a talk or training that is well received, people will come up and say, "Shona, you're amazing! What you said is amazing!"

 I thank them, smile, and practice the language of inner success. I tell myself, "Shona, your greatness lies in your hard work for this lecture, your ability to accept critique and incorporate feedback, and your humility when doing a great job."

Of course, the compliments feel good but they don't define my value. Now when my talks don't go over as well, I remind myself, "I tried my best. Let me figure out what can I learn from this for next time. My real greatness lies in my ability to learn from this and improve. I don't have control over the audience."

> **Laugh!**
> The world around us is such an unreliable barometer to assess meaningful successes and failures.
>
> As I've been teaching about these ideas, I've begun to laugh at all the funny moments that we misunderstand success and failure within our everyday life.

MEASURING OUR EFFORT

I'll never forget the day my sister won a prize for being the most altruistic and kind person in the class. She came home and told us about the prize, and of course we congratulated her. However, we couldn't help but laugh at the ridiculousness of a girl who refused to help with basic chores on Sunday could then be revered by her school on Tuesday. It often really does help to laugh.

How much effort should we put in to achieving internal success? With external success, effort is usually (but not always!) related to the needs of what we produce. We will try, try, and even try again if we want to improve the product.

But when it comes to internal success, it's so much harder to measure the required effort. It often seems as if we can always drive ourselves further, but there does come a point of diminishing returns and we need to be cautious about burnout. Here's a model that's useful in measuring just the right amount of effort in each of three areas: a comfort zone, a stretch zone, and an anxiety zone.

Comfort	Stretch	Anxiety
We're relaxed. Maybe too relaxed.	We're working out. We're strengthening our personal growth muscles. (Sweet Spot!)	We're living with stress and tension.

- When you have an internal mindset, you should mostly be in **stretch mode**. You want to stretch your inner qualities and challenge yourself to grow in every circumstance.

- At times, we need comfort mode to reenergize. However, being in **comfort zone** for long periods of time usually speaks to a more passive nature. We don't want to be underachievers—in danger of shortchanging our personal development.

- Inevitably, there will be some situations of anxiety while we stretch ourselves in more difficult and challenging situations. However, we should never be in **anxiety** modes for long periods of time—that's usually symptomatic of an unhealthy overachieving mindset.

PRACTICE GETTING FIT

For external achievements, success is usually apparent: You either achieved something or you didn't. Internal success, on the other hand, is much harder to measure. It's an ongoing lifelong process.

We like results. We like to know we've accomplished something. I've found it helpful to notice the small, incremental successes along the long road to growth using the FIT principle.

Frequency

Intensity

Time

There are three basic questions to consider when using FIT to measure your progress:

Frequency: How often does this show up? Is it getting more or less frequent? The frequency of character defects popping up for a quick "hello" is a great way to measure how much progress you're making. On the flip side, you can look at how frequently you are showing your best character development.

Wow, I only got angry once this week. I was able to let three comments go without reacting.

It was great, I only blamed others twice. I was able to own up to what I did twice this week.

I really struggled to show empathy three times, but I was able to show empathy the last time we met.

Intensity: How intense was this reaction?

How intensely was I impatient? Did I yell, shout, blame others?

How intensely was I angry? Did I yell, fight, say things I feel bad about?

How rigid was I? Was I unable to give two minutes of my time, or simply take a different route home, or wait the extra five minutes in line?

Time: How long did it last?

Did I catch myself after a minute or two and change course?

Was I able to apologize right after I was wrong?

Did I take deep breaths and accept what I couldn't change after just a few minutes of resentment?

Using these reflection questions will help you measure the progress you're making toward your goals. It won't be tomorrow, and probably not next week, but, as Mr. Rogers famously said, "Discovering the truth about ourselves is a lifetime's work, but it's worth the effort."[28]

Here's an example. Dave was working on being a more giving person. Each week, he discussed with Yael the actions he had taken to improve. Looking at FIT, Dave was able to self-assess his own successes and failures—even when he felt discouraged. Dave struggled to give to others when he wasn't benefiting, but he noticed that he was now starting to give a little bit more, with greater care and for longer periods of time. FIT helped him measure his successes and also assess the work that lay ahead.

One of my own internal challenges is to not be so impatient. This book challenged my ability to improve in this area. Learning to be more persistent and patient is an incredible effort! At times, I wasn't sure if I was actually making any progress, so I used the FIT principle to see how I was doing.

I noticed I was persistent in the face of impatience more often, and the intensity and length of my impatience was reduced most of the time. I wasn't perfect—as clearly seen from the dozens of small moments that I felt impatient and unwilling to edit again, and again. But using the FIT principle, I could see my improvement and celebrate my successes.

COGNITIVE BEHAVIOR THERAPY (CBT)

Cognitive Behavioral Therapy is about changing the way you think (cognitive) as well as what you do (behavior). CBT starts by helping to identify troubling situations or conditions in your life. Once you become aware of your thoughts, emotions, and beliefs about these problems, you can then identify negative or inaccurate thinking and reshape it to be more useful for you.[29]

Changes in thinking and action don't happen overnight—they require practice. Many CBT programs include homework and language practice. The importance of practice, the research shows, is that the more familiar you are with the new way of thinking and behaving, the more likely it is to impact real change in your life. If you practice with small issues, you are more likely to use the same behavior in more significant moments, which is when real change that will occur.

CHAPTER EIGHT

THE JOURNEY STARTS NOW

After 18 months, Yasmin called it quits.

This wasn't the way things were supposed to be. Yasmin was a high-powered Type A, who graduated at the top of her class from business school. Both Yasmin and her husband presumed that their lives would default to prioritizing her career. After all, Yasmin was a rockstar.

And for a while, that's what happened. Yasmin got a series of quick promotions, as expected. Then she decided to pursue her passion for education and dedicate her life to the startup of her dreams. She had the money, the connections, and the experience to succeed.

Now, reality was not matching expectations. Not only was the start-up struggling—as all startups do—but Yasmin faced a series of personal challenges that were just too much to handle. The bottom line was Yasmin couldn't make her startup work.

"This wasn't the right thing," Yasmin told me. "Once I looked at the balance of my personal life, alongside this driving feeling that I needed to be a CEO, I realized that my life just isn't working. I couldn't quite cancel my kids, so I canceled my role as CEO.

"And now, I feel like I'm a failure. I've never been a failure! I'm good at everything I do. This is a gut wrenching feeling."

Yasmin decided she would still attend many of the meetings she'd set up to develop important connections. One of those meetings changed her life.

During coffee with a leading Silicon Valley venture capitalist, Yasmin repeated her story. She ended by expressing disappointment in the failure she had become and thanked the gentleman for his time. Then, he said something that completely shocked her.

"Yasmin, I just want you to know that I very rarely fund a venture that hasn't had a founder that experienced at *least* one failure."

That stopped Yasmin dead in her tracks. It was at that moment that she realized failure isn't a destination, it's just a way stop on the journey.

Let's face it. Failure on any level is difficult to accept. It's incredibly disappointing—sometimes even gut wrenching. It's always just plain hard. But, if you let failure define you, then you're letting the world define you. The same thing is true for external success. It always feels amazing—sometimes in large ways and sometimes in small ones. But when you are defined by that success, you're also letting the world define you. When you're intrinsically motivated and internal essence focused, then you'll use failed experiences as growth opportunities. And external success will feel great—but they won't become the definition of who you are.

When you live a life of internal success, life is no longer driven by what other people think. Your life becomes about you. As does your growth. And your authentic development. And your expanding definition of self and personal growth.

When you live a life of internal success, life is no longer driven by what other people think.

THIS IS JUST THE START OF THE CONVERSATION. IT'S A CONSTANT RECALIBRATION.

Consider my daily self-talk while I was writing this book. On one hand, I would constantly be amazed at how life changing it's been—what an incredibly fulfilling and happy life it's given me! Surely, this will speak to others and my messages will resonate.

Then, just a few minutes later, I'd agonize over the outcome: What will people think? Will they like it? Will it improve their life? Will the book find success? What if *not a single person* reads it after all this effort?

What will this say about me? What will it mean about my work?

That's the struggle.

LIVING A LIFE OF INTERNAL SUCCESS

We know that the conversation we've had till now is no longer working.

We live in anxiety.

We live in depression.

We live in more anxiety.

We live in inadequacy.

We live in competition.

We live in *even more* anxiety.

We worry so much about what other people think. About how we're perceived. About whether we look successful.

But life is a journey, not a destination. When we see ourselves through the lens of internal essence and focus on achieving internal successes, we can recognize where to put our efforts. And when we do that, we can really start living as our best selves.

A few years ago, I trekked a really difficult hike. Maybe you, too, have had this experience. As you're walking, you almost feel like you can't make it one step further. You pause to take a drink of water or to have a snack and rest in the shade. Every step during the second half of the hike feels arduous and impossible. Finally, you get to the top, look down at the view, and you're amazed.

What I saw that day was a gorgeous waterfall which, at that exact moment, had a crisp clear rainbow overhead. The view nearly took my breath away. I couldn't get enough photos or videos to capture the awesomeness of that moment. It was worth every step of the difficult journey.

I promised you that this wasn't the usual self-help book, but rather a book about reality. Consider this. Life is the hike itself.

That awesome view—the one that almost takes your breath away— that's the halfway mark. But there are also the moments you get stuck gasping for air and realize that you should rest in the shade. There are the moments that you feel depleted and demoralized, and you wonder if you're going to be able to keep going. There's also that moment that you look around, gather your belongings, and decide to just keep putting one foot in front of the other and try to keep going to the next vista.

LEARNING TO LOVE OURSELVES

My mother famously tells the story of me as a four-year-old. She took me out of the bath, cuddled me tight, and said, "I love you so much!" I looked joyous so she continued, "Grandma and Grandpa love you, Bubby and Zeidy love you, Auntie Jo and Uncle Dave, Uncle Michael and Auntie Diana, they all love you!"

The list went on, and with each name my joy seemed to have continued. My mother mentioned the name of each of my siblings, and I smiled. When she finished the list, I glowingly looked at my mother and said, "And I even love myself!"

If only, I think to myself, I owned those words every day of my teenage life—and through adulthood too!

When we rise above the focus of our external realities and see them as vehicles to our internal success, self-acceptance becomes achievable. And with real self-acceptance comes authentic self-esteem and true happiness.

Ultimately, as Carol Dweck highlights in *Mindset*, it's about process over product. It's about remembering where our real control lies and ensuring that we place all our self-value and self-love in that truth.

FREEDOM

Imagine this. Living a life where you don't have to worry about what other people think. Living a life where you don't have to be consumed by the anxiety of external success, expectations, and failures. Living a life where you seize control of what's yours to own, and let go of what's not. That's freedom. That's a liberating way of living that frees up your mental, physical, and psychological space.

What I've come to realize in life is that by focusing only on that which is in my control—my internal essence—gives me so much mental freedom and space

When I'm not consumed by anxieties about the outcome of my children, my situation at work, and whether or not people will look at me and think I'm successful enough or smart enough or attractive enough, I have so much more time and mental space available for the world around me.

When I'm not obsessively checking social media and comparing, posting, or worrying about how successful I look, I'm always at peace internally.

It doesn't mean that I always feel this way. For example, there are the days that I take flights.

I hate flying. Talk about a series of processes out of your control! How bad will the traffic be to the airport? How frequently does the shuttle bus comes to the parking lot? How long are the security and check-in lines. And, of course, will my flight be on time or delayed?

Boy, does my anxiety kick into full gear! On days when I fly, I might have two hours until I need to leave for the airport, but I can barely get a single thing done because I'm too busy worrying.

But then I remember where my control lies. I remember that all I can do is stay focused on my inner essence. On those days, or in those moments, I live a life with so much availability to focus less on myself and more on contributing to others in the world around me.

You can do this too.

Consider for just a moment how much of your day is focused on things outside of your control—whether it's your physical responsibilities or your mental space. Now, imagine that you clear that memory and free up all those brain cells. I bet you, too, will find lots of extra time, space, and mental energy.

Now, imagine that you take all that extra mental energy and use it to think about ways to improve your life—to give to others and to think about ways to keep feeling whole and happy.

Pretty incredible, huh?

That's what a life of internal success will do for you, just as it's done for me.

ULTIMATELY, MAKE YOUR LIFE MATTER

Now, dear reader, you have in your hands the tools to make these changes happen. Anxiety doesn't have to be the narrative of your world. Imperfection and mediocrity don't have to be the bane of your existence. Inadequacy doesn't have to drive your choices and personal feelings. Fear of failure doesn't have to limit you or define you.

These feelings won't be banished forever. They'll regularly crop up and you'll have to visit with them occasionally. But when they do, you'll know exactly how to walk them to the door and slam it shut behind them.

WHERE DO YOU GO FROM HERE?

So, you've got the tools. What will you do with them?

To help you on your journey (and remember, inner success is a journey, not a destination), I've created a companion journal, with 52 thoughts, ideas, and activities to keep you engaged in internal success work for the next year

It's sometimes easy to imagine that you have to travel to the Himalayas in Tibet or the ashram in India or the rice fields of Bali to find serenity and happiness.

I've been to some of those places and let me share a secret: What you need is already inside of you. Just like Dorothy in *The Wizard of Oz*, you have everything you need around you.

Enjoy the journey.

ABOUT THE AUTHOR

Shona Schwartz is a school principal with over a decade of experience building curricula of excellence in academic and Social Emotional Learning. With classroom teaching experience from kindergarten through college level, Shona has worked with thousands of students and dozens of educators across the world to think innovatively about designing educational environments that foster a deep sense of success, fulfillment, and resilience for students based on the internal success concepts.

In addition to her classroom teaching, Shona has consulted with educational institutions, spoken at conferences, and worked with Fortune 500 companies sharing ways to help people internalize their own authentic power and self-worth. From student homework to the manager's desk, Shona works with clients to build environments that foster internal success to support individuals to take greater risks, build resilience, and maintain independent personal value in the face of success and failure.

ACKNOWLEDGEMENTS

I am eternally grateful to all the people who have helped me shape my career and build my expertise, and to all those who supported me in my decade-long process to publish this book. First and foremost is my mother, Yael, whose life's work is found in each page of these chapters, and whose parenting is the bedrock of my fulfilling and happy life.

Thank you to all those who, over the last decade, listened to me complain, get frustrated, inspired, excited, and frustrated again in my talk about "my book on internal success." Devora—you are a true friend. The amount of support and edits you've offered over the last decade has made this entire project possible.

I am so grateful for all the educational teams, supervisors, administrators, and clients who have taught me so much over the last few years. A special thank you to my team at Wornick—Barbara, Nicole, and Joel—who believed in me when I was younger and dumber than I realized. A special thank you to Melissa, who forever changed my life by introducing me to *Mindset* by Carol Dweck and who has remained a supportive friend—wherever I live. To the teams at all the schools I work at and my clients across Palo Alto, Singapore, NY, NJ, and elsewhere: I would not be where I am today without your insights, experiences, and opportunities.

To all the thought leaders and influencers who were willing to meet with me and support my work many years ago—especially Carol Dweck and Adam Grant—your feedback was especially helpful in guiding me and encouraging me to shape this project.

Thanks to all the people who helped make this book a reality by proofreading, suggesting edits, and driving it to completion: Linda Popky, my patient, tolerant, and amazing editor (and more!), Aba, and so many friends and colleagues over the years who read drafts and gave feedback.

To the one who really made this rewrite happen—the bedrock of our family and my everything—my husband, Eli. You continuously inspire me to try and try again, and to never let failure be an excuse for not trying yet again. Your edits, feedback, constant support, and own authorship are the reasons the book is here today. Again.

To my kids—Gavriel, Ariel, Ilan, and Daniel: I hope we inspire you to be men of internal success and to develop into the best version of yourselves. I love you.

END NOTES

1. Wendy Mogul, *Blessings of a Skinned Knee: Using Jewish Teachings to Raise Self-Reliant Children* (New York: Simon and Schuster Publishing, 2008).
2. Bob Brown, "Wellesley Grads told You're Not So Special," 2012, https://theswellesleyreport.com/2012/06/wellesley-high-grads-told-youre-not-special/.
3. "Barney – Everyone is Special," Songlyrics.com, accessed June 30, 2022, https://www.songlyrics.com/barney/everyone-is-special-lyrics/.
4. Multiple intelligences is a theory developed by Howard Garner that highlights the various ways in which people may be intelligent.
5. Patricia Cross, "Not Can, But Will College Teaching Be Improved?" *New Directions for Higher Education* 1977, no. 17 (1977): 1–15.
6. "It's Academic," 2000. *Stanford GSB Reporter*, April 24, pp. 14–5. via Zuckerman (2001). "What Makes You Think You're So Popular? Self-Evaluation Maintenance and the Subjective Side of the 'Friendship Paradox'?" *Social Psychology Quarterly* 64, no.3: 207–223.
7. Michael McQueen, "The Dark Side of Self-Esteem: the 5 unintended consequences of giving too much praise & affirmation," https://michaelmcqueen.net/category/23-for-parents-and-teachers?download=90.
8. *Collins Dictionary*, "Average," accessed June 30, 2022, https://www.collinsdictionary.com/dictionary/english/average#:~:text=An%20average%20is%20the%20result,of%20numbers%20you%20added%20together.
9. Saxby Pridmore and Anil Reddy, "Financial loss and suicide," *The Malaysian Journal of Medical Sciences: MJMS* vol. 19,2 (2012): 74–6. https://www.ncbi.nlm.nih.gov/pmc/articles/PMC3431736/.
10. Marshall Goldsmith, *The Earned Life: Lose Regret, Choose Fulfillment* (New York: Currency Books, 2022).
11. Berns, Sam. *My Philosophy for a Happy Life*, TED, December 2013, https://www.ted.com/talks/sam_berns_my_philosophy_for_a_happy_life.

12. Patrick Frye, "U.S. Military Enlistment Recruiters Reject 71 Percent of Applicants for Army, Navy, Marines, and Air Force," Inquisitr, June 29, 2014, https://www.inquisitr.com/1324635/u-s-military-enlistment-recruiters-reject-71-percent-of-applicants-for-army-navy-marines-and-air-force/.

13. Stephen R. Covey, *The 7 Habits of Highly Effective People: Restoring the Character Ethic* (New York: Free Press, 2004).

14. Maria, Konnikova, *The Biggest Bluff: How I Learned to Pay Attention, Master Myself, and Win* (New York: Penguin Press, 2020).

15. *Race to Nowhere*, Vicki Abeles, Jessica Congdon, Maimone Attia, Sophia Constantinou, and Mark Adler, Netflix, 2010.

16. Chris Kenrick, "In new classes, students explore the brighter side," *Palo Alto Online*, February 2014, https://www.paloaltoonline.com/news/2014/02/21/students-explore-the-brighter-side-in-new-classes.

17. Ellen Langer, "The Illusion of Control," *Journal of Personality and Social Psychology*, 32, no.2 (1975): 311–328. https://doi.org/10.1037/0022-3514.32.2.311.

18. Po Bronson, "How Not To Talk To Your Kids," *New York Magazine*, February 2007, https://nymag.com/news/features/27840/.

19. Dr. Becky Kennedy, "Dr. Becky at Good Inside," Facebook, retrieved March 2021, https://m.facebook.com/drbeckyatgoodinside/photos/a.103672637919627/263256588627897/?type=3&_rdr.

20. Adam Grant, *Give and Take: A Revolutionary Approach to Success* (New York: Viking, 2013).

21. Carol Dweck, "Caution—Praise Can Be Dangerous," 1999, https://www.aft.org/sites/default/files/periodicals/PraiseSpring99.pdf.

22. Stephanie Rosenbloom, "But Will It Make You Happy?" New York Times, August 7, 2010, retrieved August 16, 2010. https://www.nytimes.com/2010/08/08/business/08consume.html.

23. Ibid.

24. Amanda MacMillan, "Why Instagram Is the Worst Social Media for Mental Health," *Time Magazine*, 2017, https://time.com/4793331/instagram-social-media-mental-health/.

25. Alfie Kohn, *No Contest: The Case Against Competition* (New York: Houghton Mifflin, 1992).

26. Malcolm Gladwell, *Outliers: The Story of Success* (New York: Back Bay Books, 2011).

27. Bruno Bettelheim, *A Good Enough Parent: A Book on Child-Rearing*, (New York: Vintage, 1988).

28. Fred Rogers, Quotable Quote, https://www.goodreads.com/quotes/156148-discovering-the-truth-about-ourselves-is-a-lifetime-s-work-bu, retrieved June 30, 2022.

YOUR INTERNAL
SUCCESS JOURNAL

As we know, internal success is a continual work in progress. Some days, this feels so achievable, while at other moments, it can feel so overwhelming. The goal of this journal is to create a space for you to chart your progress in the stretch zone, to recognize when you're hanging out too long in the comfort or anxiety mode, and to recalibrate as needed. It's intended to support you as you move down this path, putting one foot in front of the other.

Don't think you need to journal every day, or even every week. This should not be a stressful or anxious process. The last thing that I want to do is give you a rigid set of directions that might keep you in the anxiety zone. Rather, these prompts are here to help you to think about and reflect on where you are, so you can take action to remain in the stretch zone as much as possible.

I've laid this out as a 52-week journal, but of course, take this at your own pace. You'll see as you go through the journal—when you welcome these prompts into your life—you'll reflect upon them with the mindset of where you are at that time. There's no right way to do this. It's your journey.

Have a wonderful journey.

WEEK 1

How am I? Write about how you're feeling right now: About this whole process. About internal and external success. About control and lack of control. About competitiveness and specialness.

WEEK 2

What are five things that made you feel special this week? Were they internal or external? When you look at that list, can you identity what's external and what's internal?

WEEK 3

Where did you feel competitive this week?
How do you manage that?

WEEK 4

What was one time this week you noticed yourself
feeling valued for your external realities?

WEEK 5

Write about one time this week when you noticed
yourself thinking about internal and external success.
What were your thoughts? Did they further your
self-value based on internal essence, or did you feel
uncertain about your personal value?

WEEK 6

Where did you put effort this week that didn't give you the results wanted? How did you respond to that disappointment?

WEEK 7

What is one risk you took this week—big or small—
that you took this week because you were able to
hold your inner essence and jump into an external
challenge feeling confident and strong inside?

WEEK 8

Write about one moment on social media that you reframed. What was troubling you and how did you reframe it to balance realities of internal and external success?

WEEK 9

What one thing out of your control did you accept this
week? How did you come to a place of acceptance?
What was the result of that letting go?

WEEK 10

What moment of anxiety did you have this week?
How did you consider the control factor
in figuring out what you were able to do
and what you had to let go?

WEEK 11

*Think about one time when you were
criticized or complimented this week that
felt good. How did you view this criticism
or compliment in light of internal and
external realities?*

WEEK 12

Write an internal success you
had in a relationship this week.

_____

_____

_____

_____

_____

_____

_____

_____

_____

_____

_____

WEEK 13

What was your favorite internal
success moment this week?

WEEK 14

*What external success did you have this week
that you were able to celebrate, but still
recognize as an external success?*

WEEK 15

*Write about something that happened this week
where you really struggled to hold on to your inner
essence while you felt the strong pull of external
things. How did you navigate that struggle?*

WEEK 16

Write about your favorite moment this week,
where you found yourself placing your self-value
in inner essence, and actually noticing it this
week and giving yourself a pat on the back.

WEEK 17

What moment this week made you laugh about
our weird, externally driven world?

WEEK 18

This week is about freedom of thought.
What's on your mind? What areas are working?
What feels like an ongoing challenge? Where are you
starting to see the fruits of your labor?

WEEK 19

*What has required the most effort in this
journey towards internal success? How are you
celebrating yourself for those efforts?*

WEEK 20

What is your most cherished outcome of this new you and your new life? Write about a moment when you breathed a deep, fulfilling breath, and thought, OMG, it's working!

WEEK 21

Write about a goal you're working on this week.
What parts of your internal essence are you
stretching for this goal? What part of the outcome
of this goal is out of your control?

WEEK 22

Write about a victory you had over a moment
of anxiety this week. What thoughts went through
your mind as you fought those feelings of
anxiety and "flipped the script"?

WEEK 23

*How has your work on internal success had a positive
impact on your life or on your relationship with
others. Think of the large, more obvious examples,
and the smaller, more mundane moments.*

WEEK 24

Sometimes growth is two steps forward, one step back. Take a moment to recognize your efforts over these past few weeks. Journal what feels relevant to the jaggedness that is growth. Perhaps draw an image, or chart the ups and downs.

WEEK 25

Draw a circle of control around your life this week.
What's happening that's in your control and what
in reality is completely outside of the circle?

WEEK 26

If you were giving yourself an award for
Best Internal Success, what would the award
be and what have you done to receive it?

WEEK 27

*Write about a courageous moment when
you caught yourself accepting the things you
cannot change, and you were able to channel
the courage to change the things you could.*

WEEK 28

Write about one time this week when you shifted
from externally driven to internally driven language
(either directed to yourself or to others).

WEEK 29

Write about one moment this week when
you took time to celebrate your growth.

WEEK 30

What one moment this week felt hard?
Very, very hard.

WEEK 31

Write one affirmation that speaks to the internal essence that motivates you. What's your favorite thing to say to yourself as a motivator to keep up the internal success mindset?

WEEK 32

What is one example of an external reality
that improved as a result of your work
on your internal essence?

WEEK 33

What one thing you read, saw, or heard this week
that made you think about internal success?

WEEK 34

What inspiring quote have you found that
speaks to the value of internal success?

WEEK 35

Write about an external failure or success
that brought up a lot of strong feelings for you.
Validate that. Process that. Then challenge
yourself to remember: My value is in
my internal essence.

WEEK 36

*Evaluate your week. What were your greatest
moments of anxiety? Looking deeper, were
these fueled by themes of control, inadequacy,
or external realities? Reflect on that.*

_____

_____

_____

_____

_____

_____

_____

_____

_____

_____

_____

WEEK 37

What language of internal success were you
able to use this week—either directed
to yourself or to others?

WEEK 38

*Write down a mantra for the week. This could
be about serenity prayer, control, or what
internal essence makes me special.*

WEEK 39

Say into the mirror: I am an amazing,
average person. What is that like for you?
How does it feel?

WEEK 40

What advice have you recently gotten that gave you a feeling of anxiety. Reflect on that feeling. Was the advice competitively driven? Was it externally driven? What about it felt uncomfortable to you?

WEEK 41

Think about putting process over product. Write about one process where you're actively engaged (internal or external). How's it going?

WEEK 42

What one thing have you done or will you do this
week to nurture self-love and acceptance?

WEEK 43

What makes you proud this week?

WEEK 44

Write about a mistake you've made recently that you were able to turn into a learning experience.

WEEK 45

What happened this week that caused you
to think, "Wow! I'm seeing change?"

WEEK 46

Describe a moment of happiness you had recently. What made you happy?

WEEK 47

Reflect on a moment of competition that didn't feel great. What strategies did you employ to confront that discomfort?

WEEK 48

Write about something for which you received
a compliment. Did you actually put a lot of
effort into this? How did you feel if you
didn't put out a lot of effort?

WEEK 49

Write about something for which you were criticized.
What did you take away from this that you will be
able to use and reflect upon in a helpful way?

WEEK 50

Complete this sentence:

My favorite part of this journey has been . . .

WEEK 51

Complete this sentence:

The most difficult part of this journey has been . . .

WEEK 52

Complete this sentence:
The mantras I now live by are . . .

_____

_____

_____

_____

_____

_____

_____

_____

_____

_____

_____

_____

_____

WEEK 53

Congratulations! You've completed 52 weeks of
internal success work. Write down how you feel.
What feels right? What still needs attention?
What will you work on next?

Made in the USA
Monee, IL
25 June 2023

37369827R00163